Libraries
ReadLearnConnect

THIS BOOK IS PART OF ISLINGTON READS BOOKSWAP SCHEME

Please take this book and either return it to a Bookswap site or replace with one of your own books that you would like to share.

If you enjoy this book, why not join your local Islington Library and borrow more like it for free?

Find out about our FREE e-book, e-audio, newspaper and magazine apps, activities for pre-school children and other services we have to offer at www.islington.gov.uk/libraries

ISLINGTON
For a more equal future

ARACHNE PRESS

First published in UK 2014 by Arachne Press Limited
100 Grierson Road, London SE23 1NX
www.arachnepress.com
© Arachne Press 2014
ISBN: 978-1-909208-18-6
Edited by Cherry Potts
The moral rights of the authors have been asserted
All content is copyright the respective authors.
For copyright on individual poems see page 3.

All rights reserved. This book is sold subject to the condition
that it shall not by way of trade or otherwise, be lent, resold,
hired out or otherwise circulated without the publisher's prior
written consent in any form or binding or cover other than
that in which it is published and without similar condition
including this condition being imposed on the subsequent
purchaser.
Except for short passages for review purposes no part of this
publication may be reproduced, stored in a retrieval system or
transmitted in any form, or by any means, electronic,
mechanical, photocopying, recording or otherwise without
prior written permission of Arachne Press.
Printed on wood free paper in the UK by TJ International,
Padstow.

Individual Copyright

A Visitation at the Abbey of Barking © Judi Sutherland 2014

Bewcastle Point to Point © Geraldine Green 2014

Compass © Carl Griffin 2014

Eris Speaks © Cathy Bryant 2014

Faith in a Time of Double-dip Recessions © Inua Ellams
originally published in *The Morning Star* 2014

Graffiti © Elinor Brooks 2014

Grass Was Taller © j.lewis 2014

Grithspell © Math Jones 2014

Hamnavoe © Andrew McCallum originally published as an audio
recording in *Samplings* 2014

I Have No Feet © Bernie Howley 2014

I Went to the Market… © Anne Macaulay 2014

In Retail (xxiii) © Jeremy Dixon 2014

Lïr © Angela France originally published in *Long Poem Magazine*
winter 2009/10

Naming: AD 2006 © Alwyn Marriage 2006

On the Hunt with Mr Actaeon © Jill Sharp 2014

Orion © Simon Brod 2014

Revenant © Sarah Lawson 2014

Rhythms © Adrienne Silcock 2011

Robinson © Brian Johnstone originally published by Akros
Publications in 2000

The Black Light Engineer © p.a.morbid 2014

The Broken Thread © Robin Winckel-Mellish 2014

The Other Side of Sleep © Kate Foley 2014

Time Travel © Sam Small 2014

Troy: Seven Voices © Jennifer A. McGowan originally published
in *Envoi* 2010

Voices After a Tsunami © Emma Lee sections of this poem
appeared in *Ink Sweat and Tears* 2013 this version 2014

CONTENTS

THE OTHER SIDE OF SLEEP
Kate Foley

'It's a profession, you know…'
Tracy Groom wafts a hand at her framed Diploma:

Certified Dream Walker:
        Death Coach.

Basil's freckles shift, small brown islands
on his too thin skin. He frowns.

'Coach? Sounds like plumes
and black horses to me.'

Ms Groom – she rarely owns to Tracy –
deepens her eyes. 'How long?'

Basil shrugs. 'Could be months.'
 'Loved ones who might need extra care?'

Terry had died when AIDS was nameless,
before this out/proud/new-fangled partner stuff

came in and Basil embraced Respectable
as if she were a muse. 'No one' he grunts.

Tracy is shrewd as a cat in a bush
full of birds. She waits.

'What is it exactly you think I might –
might – be able to do for you?'

But Basil, who found his fatal lump
when pleasuring himself stiffly,

who's suffered diagnosis
and the indignities of failed cure,

as a paid-up dug-in crustacean, won't admit
his internet trawl of Death,

or how the phrase Dream Walker
reminds him of cowboys and indians,

of black and white films flickering,
short grey trousers and innocence.

Mr Catullus, a ginger cat slumbers fatly
on a window ledge ripe with potted marigolds.

'Why is everything orange?' asks Basil.
'Gold' she says 'the colour of the lining of fear.'

'The lining of fear?' 'Don't say 'sounds like' –
do yourself a courtesy – let the meaning sink in.'

'Oh – there's a meaning is there, then?' Basil's
identity in its little round shell house, burrows.

Truculence, a word coined for him,
fattens his lower lip.

'You used to teach woodwork, I believe?'
A grudging nod.

'Then you must know
how much skill and care you need to make

a chair, even a box. Why grudge the care
you need to craft the house your spirit

needs to die in?' 'What's
all this Indian stuff then?' Basil demands.

'Why can't Death...' – he gives it a capital
to show he's not scared – 'be English?'

'So, why come to me? You knew The Eternal Flame
has links with the Elder Wisdom.'

But she can't keep up the warrior-for-truth stance.
It's the way his moustache –

that little dickey-bow of hair under his nose –
wobbles. 'Come on, give it a try. Up on the couch!'

Basil wakes later from the deepest sleep he's ever known.
Ms Groom, was she still going on about Atlantis

and caves when sleep fell on him
like a heavy animal?

'Dreams?'
'What dreams?' Basil yawns.

'Went out like a light.
No dreams.'

It's winter. Basil's death has grown,
white and quiet as a whisker of frost.

Still no dreams, or none
he'll tell...

*Dying, when it's not snatch-and-grab, is like the walk you used
to do in minutes taking hours. Tracy's amber-bead brigade no
longer wants to pay – recession. She's 'caring' now.
Basil and Tracy, a prickly, hard green bud of – maybe
– trust?*

... but Tracy, obstinate as ever,
still hopes, still chants,

still watches his deep, unfathomable sleep
as if he were written

in ancient undeciphered script.
'My Sleeping Tablet' his pet name for her.

They're both eroding, gently,
his life, her fierce certainties.

She watches him, unlovely, yellow
as old cabbage,

dribble on his chin. Silently, she begs him
dream. He sleeps her faith away.

 Under her breath she invokes Running Hare
Leaping Deer.

These mythical beasts are shy of Basil's
resolute slumber.

Though dreamless, blessed in the dark
halls of sleep, Basil must sometimes

between deep and shallow,
wake to memory.

Had he been a gardener wood might have bent
and bloomed for him. A kind of blossom

once curled from the plane, the smooth, dense
left-behind of made-by-hand,

close as he ever came to leaf or bud.
How can you dream of sawdust?

But pine, yellow or white, or the rich
rose coloured dust of mahogany,

Basil dreams their drift on the floor,
in the clean smell of resin –

and bees thread through his sleep,
tiny saws.

Irritably he swats his forehead.
'Pests!' he mumbles. 'What?'

'Bees' 'Where?' 'In my workshop.
Must've left the window...'

Bees? He's been dreaming!
Such rich symbolism!

Stands for immortality...
The Great Mother... messages...

she knew if she waited...
'Bas?' She spoons his soup.

'Those bees you dreamt...'
'Give it a rest, Trace. I told you,

not dreamed, remembered.'

Yes, he remembers all right,
the buzz of conversation,

blokes with their pecs straining
check shirts, their small moustaches

wet with beer. A juke box,
men dancing. First time ever

he's seen all those tight bums
waggling – men laughing

as if they felt entitled, kissing?
Basil feels as if his shirt, his tash,

his new-grown muscles, weeks of preparation,
are only borrowed.

Headlong he flees. Gets tangled
in the door. 'Hey. Where so fast?'

Ah... Terry.

Enough years. Sweet and sour domestic
plod, the rows when Terry strayed,

the healing nights, the garden shaved,
sink scrubbed, school taught, Terry's haute cuisine

when neighbours came – all swept
away, his puzzled navy eyes,

the drip, the sores, the stink and at the last,
Basil's only act of heroism,

he clambers on the hospital bed
and holds his lover in his arms.

Basil, drifting now to the sound of bees
won't allow he's dreamed,

13

knows he knows how to die.
He only needs a witness.

Bee-light
blown egg
wing-shucked

Tracy sees
eyeballs
quiver

cheeks twitch
mouth
grow soft

She makes the fire up.
Scarlet flames stitch the dark

behind her eyes. Her lids close.
The subdued tweet and whistle

of Basil's breath threads the cavern
of her ears,

                she's turning, turning,

her fingertips graze a rough,wet wall.
Her feet – she doesn't think it strange –

are luminous. This is a dancing floor
all she has to do – obey.

She thinks of her mother's button-box,

that time she threw it down,
how all the little lives of buttons

scattered and she wasn't sorry
and now she is.

'Oh! Don't cry' says a voice, deep
as a coal mine.

A smell,

concentration of deep salt, fruit, blood, wine, shit,
and yes, roses.

Tracy steals up to the figure of a seated man
– is it a he? – and presses his bare nipple.

'No, my dear. You can't light me up.
I'm not your actual electric torch.'

'Who are you, then?' 'They call me Asterion
but I've never seen one.' 'One what?'

'A Star.' In the feeble light
Tracy sees his big, mild bull's head appear.

His eyes are milky, one of his horns is chipped
and on his forehead a broken white star,

matted and bruised. She points.??...
'That was the stunner when they tried it last'

'Why?' 'Because you can't kill death
but they keep on trying.'

'Is that what I'm trying to do?'

'How would I know?
I've only seen your feet.'

A passion of pure sorrow grips Tracy
in some bodily cave she didn't know she had.

She lifts her arms above her head,
begins to dance.

When she is done
she asks 'Can I stroke you?'

'OH PLEASE'

'Ohhhhhhh Tracy.....quick!' Basil
wants to be sick. Can't wait...pain...

black bile, all over the bed. Find a bowl,
find a cloth, find a phone...

'No doctor' 'Yes! ... the pain...
I can't help you.' Tracy in firelight

and shadow has grown. Basil's afraid.
The speed, the gear-less, brakeless speed.

'Not like this' he groans. Tracy
sits behind him like a large pillow.

One hand cups his head.
The other, delicate

and strong as a resting bird
sends wordless messages to his tight fist

grasping for air. It opens slowly.
Is he held? Do we know?

Poetry or prayer can only take you so far.

Tracy lets tomorrow's light
wash her face
like a morning cat.

Now she knows
where death and its dreams,
domestic as the tiny bones

of a child's hamster
in a shoebox,
can find its rest.

COMPASS
Carl Griffin

See the boy as a colony
of ants nesting
in the warmer side of trees
as he bends under tarp
knotted between larches
and recedes
with an imagination
we're not sturdy enough
to survive on.

Who can spy his deciduous
needle head in all those hectares?
We see a friendless child
and ten metres of timber,
then brick walls and houses
with no silence between gardens,
a closing school, supermarket,
a car-park wider
than a village.

He holds a compass,
his back to the concrete.
Everywhere there are signs
directing him North
or City Centre or the docks,
signs on every horizon
but where he looks,
his reasoning shielding
his eyes like a hand

from sun glare and panic,
the separation of a world
or a mother and father.
This might be his first
detour to Blaen-Y-Maes
having rode his bike
for miles until he happened
upon these recreational
trees, an uncharted stretch

more rural than his local milieu.
Only once the sky's pitchblende
and he steers his bike
for home, will he realise
he doesn't know the way;
You are only lost
when you know you're lost.
He is opposite to a torch
shining in daylight.

What about the two of us,
watching him as if
that compass
wouldn't feel solid
and precious
in our own palms?
Will we cycle
one morning on impulse,
rucksacks fat
 with equipment —
Swiss Army knives,
rope, First Aid,
the essentials minus
a hardback of edible berries —
and head for wherever
is greener or most different,
blistering our feet
and other vehicles?

What brought us
to each other
was no magnetic pointer
or dreamland billboard.
We share a standing cwtch
by the garden fence,
heart rhythms ominous
in bloodspills of tenderness,
security and delicious sin.

We are heading for Hell.
We don't need a compass
to tell us. But choices
for prior adventures
are all we desire,
even if we can't voice this
to a boy not daft enough
to hand his compass back
to 'those strangers', or to each other.
That zany couple Mark and Donna
drive the scenic,
mountainous route
from Skewen to Llangyfelach
after evenings out
but lack the confidence
to drive from Llangyfelach
to Skewen, via the same
road, on the way there.

This behaviour
might be teacher's distrait,
tipsily inattentive or
village idiot mimicry,
but signs aren't foolproof.
Travellers readmis them
behind heat shields
and rough weather.
Forget the junction overlooked

leading someplace magical,
which one of us — you swear
it was me — considered
not worthwhile.
Touring Aberystwyth
we met a writer
researching for a book
about the town,
its antecedents and its magnetism,

and as we looked out
to river Ystwyth
then river Rheidol
his environmental source
of brainwave and stimulation
was elementary guesswork.
But every town
has antiquity
or novelty in abundance.

I'm spooked by distance,
the vastness even
of countries the size
of Wales — perhaps due
to having never travelled
overseas — the distance
between lorry
and loading bay,
a snapdragon's spike

and the curved lip
of its flowers.
Aberystwyth's budding author
knows the market town
like the back of his hand
but I need fresh grit, the railfreight
traffic at Margam Knuckle Yard,
and all five blast furnaces
of Port Talbot's Steelworks.

Saltings in West Wales
dazzle as much
as salt marsh in the South
but the sublime, you are certain,
is in the stone roll,
and why waste dead reckoning
or celestial navigation
in the ghostly rain
of restricted waters.

Camping in Nevada
means jackrabbits,
pronghorn antelope
and bristlecone pines,
sagebrush valleys
and craggy mountains,
or canyons eroded
into bentonite clay,
or blazing red sandstone,

lava beds, playa plains
and wagon wheel ruts,
quarries, or granite cirques,
moraines, houseboats
on manmade oases.
Camping in Blaen-Y-Maes
means waking to a tethered
piebald horse
chewing your flysheet.

And outside our home
in Blaen-Y-Maes
I have to nudge you,
unsure you have woken.
We are tired from hiking
on the spot, dreaming
of surviving on sap
with the boy in his jungle,
but, leaving the garden,
we realise he has gone.

No opportunity means more
than one you just ignored.
He takes with him the compass
you gave him, and our hostility
because we couldn't work
the contraption out.
later, we magnetize
a straightened paperclip

to create a nearly
frictionless bearing,
centre it on a cork float
and watch it leisurely point
North. We realise we know
no one North of here,
or any th or st of here,
and drift back indoors
a distributary resigned to billeting.

TROY: SEVEN VOICES
Jennifer A McGowan

I. PATROCLUS

Gold is heavy,
and chafes.

Still
the fear of who I'm not
is effective,
the desperate pause
as I approach
making the thrust easy, and then
the soft sibilance
of blood on the ground.

Who'd have thought
one dice game
and a teenage crush
would lead to these endless forays
against the walls,
this skilled impersonation?

I've done more than fifty, I bet.
My arm is almost tired.
I stretch as Chiron taught us
crack my neck
and stride forward.

At last.
Hector.

II. GREEK SOLDIER

All we wanted
was to get a glimpse of her.
The one we'd come for. The one
made fools of kings
and warriors of farmers.

Each morning
before dawn
before the light could betray us
we'd scan the walls
and the tower windows
for a sight.

We never got one.
Throughout the years of fighting,
these years of boy into man
we dreamed. Silently
to each other we'd relate
our stories of her,

the way she'd look sideways
and knees that never knew fear
would buckle.
How her eyes shone like lightning and burned.

And how at the end
the one we'd all come to
we'd hear quiet footsteps
and the white fingers that closed
our eyes would be soft as featherdown
and one bright tear would be our swansong.

III. SCAMANDER

I have carried this weary leaf
from hoary mountain slopes over rocks
past thirsty roots and wading herons
past shoals of trout, silver-scaled,
to this broad plain.
Now my waters swell to flood.
Armour and keepsakes sink.
I bring the detritus of flesh
with its seeping red
to the receiving sea
where all burdens are absorbed
and nameless.

IV. ASTYANAX

Just a moment of flight
was all there was.

V. POLYXENA

Dear Achilles,

I didn't want this.
Not the fame,
not the long blue gaze
over my brother's body
that drowned us.

When I threw my bracelets down
from the tower to make up
Hector's ransom,
I was throwing you away,
knowing you'd not survive him long.

I should have known
a self-love big as yours
wouldn't rest in an easy grave.
Even dead you must get
what you want.

So I dress
as if for my wedding
while Andromache and my women
mourn. But let me tell you,
my blood
will bring you no peace.

When I fall
I will fall with the weight of Troy
and my shade's arms
around your neck
will be a millstone.

VI. CASSANDRA

Listen to me: looks aren't everything,
but they help.
Sixteen and cursed by a god—
well, that wasn't good,
but once the walls fell
and knives were everywhere,
a tear-stained and pretty face
was my ticket back to life.
A trophy's not the best option,
but as a princess, let's face it,
I was born to belong to someone,
whatever name you put on it.

I look at these new and proud owners
and see beyond them to their deaths.
Some by women's hand; some by fire;
others by neglect, as war wounds infect
and incapacitate. Agamemnon, now,
he goes home to a story
they'll be telling for years.
He's forgotten he married Helen's sister,
who comes with her own price and
a lifetime grudge of being second.

The shadows of Troy are long.
What they touch will falter.
The gods must have tragedy.
Speaking of which, my vision clouds again:
I hear screams and tears
and the thunk of the axe.
It shouldn't come as a surprise
that I'm as mortal as you are,
but, like you, I don't listen.

VII. HECUBA

Ancient bitch, empty dugs–
battling for scraps, for
the smallest thing to crunch
between blunted teeth.

You'd think, wouldn't you,
that fifty sons would be enough.
That one would be left.
Instead, pyre after pyre,
when I even got that,
and a husband cut down at the altar.
An embarrassment of corpses.

Not that I was embarrassed.
They all fought well. We weren't the invaders.
Only Paris, smitten, young,
not old enough not to pray,
believed a promise.
He always was a fool,
but he had the sweetest voice
and a smile would charm you every time.

So fifty sons dead. Good as.
My daughters? I can't bear to think.
I should have listened to Cassandra,
looked that gift horse in the mouth,
something. Anything.

But the gods
in their slanted pity
changed me to run through the night
and whine.

And I did run. To the bowels of boats,
hiding in cargo, then on land
through forests, valleys, even backyards
if the night was thick enough.
I followed the Greeks' bloody footsteps
with my own raw ones.

On these black slopes now
under a hunter's moon
I stalk their children
and howl curses
to ever darker
and more ancient gods.

GRAFFITI
Elinor Brooks

The festival is over. One by one
The statues quicken on their plinths, abandon
All repose and covering their costumes slope off
Singly or in pairs towards the pub where they
Will be a talking point. All afternoon
The actors have dissembled, standing
Stock still while people poked and teased
Or shrieking with feigned terror ran away
At the merest gesture from the figures
Sprayed into black or gold or silver painted pose.

Now there remains just one. At first
She played the part of playing a part
Rewarded the watching child with surreptitious
Wink or beckoned with one finger to another
Careful not to let her actions coincide with
Cues: people like to work out what it is
That is controlling you.

The intervals grow longer – hours not minutes
Pass, the moment never right, and children
Who gravely gaze up at her red-rimmed eyes
Set in the purest white give up
And go off after easier prey. She waits
For the summer night to look away
So that she can stretch her heavy limbs
Her eyelids heavier still, and as the milky
Morning turns to gold and dusky pink
Her mantle settles into marble folds.

The months and seasons turn. In the city square
No one remembers how the alabaster queen
Arrived among them. With yells and shouts
Children climb the creases of her clothes,
Dogs sniff her ankles, cock their legs,
Office workers gossip over lunch,
Lovers whisper secrets. None can hear
The buried heart that beats beneath her breast.

She has her lovers too – she knows them
Not by name but by the words they carve
That glow upon her stone cold skin.
Thick as dusty ink or spider thin, graffiti
Crawls across her arms and chest
And she absorbs its stain.

The trees are in full leaf once more
The festival returns with beating drums
And strings of flags are fluttering on the fence
That leans towards the sleeping statue.
Crowds cheer the clowns, shriek at the tin-foil rain
That falls on shiny upturned faces out of a sunny sky,
Applaud the jugglers and the acrobats. The world
Has turned its back on her, neglects
To check for signs of life. But on the ground
Groping between the bars to reach a coin
A boy feels a tremor run beneath his hand
And sees the pavement crack. He cries.
Under the marble sheets a woman with no voice
Struggles vainly to give birth. Her legs are tied.

HAMNAVOE
Andrew McCallum

listen
I want to tell you something ordinary

the sun was setting when I started out
his house was on the other side of the island
cows like ships were tugging the field towards night
the quick head of a hen nodded red
among the gowans
in english gowans are called daisies
a staur is a star starn are many stars
there were thirteen in the palm of the sky
when I set out walking

I was visiting a man who believed in the stories of stories
that no truth can be told fully without telling
 of the day it was learned
I am going to teach you something to prove you were
here he said
he showed me to the kitchen

it was a bachelor's kitchen
a place where only one thing is done and quietly
 in the cupboard were two plates
in the drawer two settings

he set a milkpan on the stove
into it he measured a cup of water
two spoons of coffee the colour of earth
lighting the stove he told me to stir gently
without pausing or slowing down
like calling something old from a cave.
don't stop before it enters the light or it will turn back

the work was hypnotic
the details of the room seemed to soften in their orbits
dimly I heard him ask if I could see foam yet
I could
though now I saw it as something else
I was spinning a planet now a black planet
with black oceans toiling with muddy continents
whirling from their depths
together we watched the islands converge
and hove upwards
now he said.
he cut the flame as though putting out the sun.

two cups waited on the table
he sat while I carried the pot
and this is when I learned what I need to tell

little bubbles like wooden beads boiled up as I poured
 they clung to the edges of each cup
the man leaned forward and burst them
with his finger one by one

the old women he said
believe the bubbles are eyes
we must never let them see this world

LÏR
Angela France

Humps and hints of slumped toys
  form on the chest by the door
where his dressing gown morphs
  to folded wings and curled claws;
sleeping guardian against the park,
  the playground, the casual cruelties
of schooldays. He bright-eyes
  into the darkness, stills his breathing
 as he waits for moonrise.
  It filters through the curtains,
patterns across the floor, draws
  seven-league shadows behind his shoes,
fingers across the books on the shelf.
  Watching, he turns over.

He turns over, watching
  pages fill in memory, speaks titles to himself,
knows the height and weight of each one.
  Grimms hunch behind blue covers,
shuffling sisters and witches, feathers and princes.
  Grendel lurks under a slim black spine
and Prometheus scorches the corners
  of ivory pages. Heroes and gods
fight and play, whisper in his ears

as he numbers his books, sure they pulse
with life. Words, names, enchantments
swirl around his bed until his eyes close.
He sleeps, breathes the story-soaked air;
 fables sink into his flesh and bones.

Fables sink into his flesh
  and bones fizz under his skin as he wakes.
From his window, he watches the estate.
  He sees a ravine beneath him,
a river below the road, a glimpse
  of green scales from a hood amongst
enemies who stalk the alleys, wait for prey.
  On the street, a black car prowls;
he can see its wings, ready to unlid.
  He dresses slowly, whispers new names
for each piece of uniform: *hauberk,*
  breastplate, greaves. He hefts his backpack,
weights it with books. Ready for school;
  he's not afraid anymore.

He's not afraid. No more
   hiding in the bogs where piss-stink
clings to his skin or slinking down the halls
   with his head ducked into invisibility.
He is Jason, Perseus, Beowulf;
   His enemies circle and feint, wary
of his new height. He can see gaps
   in their armour, senses where a stab
of sarcasm will wound a tender spot
   or a timely jab of humour can colour
a hard face. He doesn't need to fight;
   looks down, watches his breastplate
melt into motley, relies on his slow
   I know you smile.

I know you smiles
   away suggestions of jobs or study,
knows Story calls to him across miles
   and borders. Under his feet
a distant thrum of words rumble
   and at his back a whisper drives him on.
I saved you. I own you. He packs his life
   in a rucksack, feels the weight on his shoulders
 as a name settles on him like a cloak;
   he is Jack Green and a compass quivers
in his chest. He turns away from home
   heads east to Baba Yaga's hut,
fingers twitching at the scent of stories,
   rattle-bag hungry at his belt.

His rattle-bag's hunger
  forces through the hut's door,
ignores the rusty rattle of her iron teeth, the ember
  of her glare. He out waits her temper,
outwits her sideways creep towards
  her silver-birch broom, teases tales
from her grim memory. He hears
  of Vasilisa the Fair and Raisa's feather,
repeats the words as Baba Yaga dozes
  by the fire, makes them his. He leaves
at dawn, heads towards the morning sun
  to look for Amaterasu's cave and Uzume's
mirror; squints at the road ahead.
  He can't rest.

He can't wrest
  stories from books or screens,
can't glean tales from other tellers;
  he has to go to the cave, the woods,
the source. He trails through towns
  and villages; squares his shoulders
against pressure at his back
  like strong wind. He tells tales
for food at strangers' firesides,
  rakes through their talk for seeds
and origins, for threads to follow.
  He trembles a spirit-man's web,
sits cross-legged on red rocks
  in dreamtime.

His dream-times are filled
  with pantheons, parables
and the constant papery whisper
  that drives him on. *I saved you. I own you.*
He hears it in the hiss of the stones
  in the sweat lodge, the swish of tyres
on roads as he thumbs for lifts, the distant
  surge of waves as he walks on a cliff
where years roll under his feet.
  He doesn't notice how his skin
has tanned or the greying of his hair.
  He looks at his hands and wonders
when fingers lengthened to elegance,
  how still they are when he listens.

How still they are as they listen
  to him weaving words into stories;
men and women lured into the circle
  of his voice. He lulls with timbre
and tone, with a steady gaze
  and quiet emphasis of his long fingers.
He tells no tales to children, doesn't promise
  happy endings: the wolf eats the girl,
children die in the woods and lessons
  are learned through blood and betrayal.
He spins air into people and beasts,
  slips inside them, speaks from their throats;
the story prowls the stage, owns him.
  He becomes the story.

He becomes the story
  at arts festivals and bookish events;
his name paraded at dinner parties.
  He strides large stages, amused
at the change from firesides and small bars,
  buys linen shirts, sleeps in hotels.
CDs sell well after shows; no-one knows
  he records them with his eyes closed;
he can't be a teller without listeners
  to hold him in the story-space
where time stops and walls recede
  to a cloudy void. He finds peace
for a while, seeing an audience stunned,
  blinking in the light.

Blinking, in the night
  outside his window, a neon sign
pulses through his room, wakes him.
  He packs a bag, can't remember
what town this is. He'll recall the gig
  by the shape of the stage, the way
his voice measured the height and depth
  of the space, the taste of the stories
on his tongue, the listeners' will
  to be drawn in. He buckles his old belt,
rattle-bag gaping at his hip; there's time
  to follow a thread picked up in a bar
before his next telling. He leaves
  a woman asleep in the bed.

A woman sleeps in his bed
  most nights; magnetised to his side
by the pitched power in his voice
  and the narrow beam of his attention.
They come after an evening's telling;
  certain he holds a key to understanding,
sure he tells their life in metaphor.
  Some stay, swept along in the slipstream
of his drive, travel with him until they find
  the depth is in the story, not the man.
Fewer come as his ponytail thins to a wisp,
  his tan sallows to weather-beaten
and his rangy height becomes skinny.
  He doesn't notice.

He doesn't know this
  town; can't recall filling the theatre's stage
 with his voice, doesn't question
  the church hall or cheap bed and breakfast
He knows the stories still matter,
  lets his tone sharpen to an audience
that fidgets and whispers; he scowls
  and stalks out at the end. He's not aware
of repeating himself or of changing tales,
  forgetting names, mixing sun and moon
deities. In his room, he stares from the window;
  thinks there's something missing, it's quiet.
He lies down to fall into an empty sleep:
  there are no dreams anymore.

There are no dreams, no more
   whispers to direct his path or shape his day.
He slouches against a bar, mumbles
   about stories he knows, how slippery
they are. He grasps a man's arm,
babbles about being saved, being left.
In a hostel he tired-eyes into darkness,
   turns away from the moon's intrusion.
He wanders the streets and parks,
   takes a lawn for a stage; people edge away,
mothers gather children. He doesn't know
   how he came to this room that stinks
of piss and cabbage. All he remembers
   is humps and hints of slumped toys.

TIME TRAVEL
Sam Small

My name's Sam Small
I'm from the future
I've no time to explain but
It's vitally important that you
let me finish this sent… BANG

x 6

My name's Sam Small
I'm from the future
Let. Me. Explain.
I'm standing over six of my own dead bodies
One for each time I've travelled

There's me as a woman

The first time I travelled time
I went back to see my parents
When they were young
Some years later when
I was born in that time line
I came out a lady
I don't know what I changed
but it must have been significant
I did make a pretty hot lady though
Always kinda did think I would
So no surprises there.

The second time I travelled time
I went back again
I met my own mum when she was pregnant with me
Strange feeling, seeing a bump that I used to occupy
 I said hello,
asked her if she was excited for the pregnancy
She said she was
They had been trying for a while and
Thought I might have been impossible
She asked me what my name was
"you don't want to know"
Said that I looked familiar
"I'm sure we'll meet soon"
That changed me again, made me taller, broader
Look a lot more like my father than my mother
Don't know what part of the meetings made
each of the changes
It's not an exact science
But I continued to travel

The third time I travelled time
I went back to the beginning
Right to beginning
Trying to prove that god never existed
I did meet a carpenter called Jesus
But didn't see any miracles
He said it was timing

It was my own fault for getting there late
But it's ok if you missed them
Cause his 12 pals over there were writing
a book about him
He said it didn't matter,
Even if I had seen them I'd still want more proof
He said I love you Sam,
and I know you've travelled a long way
But sometimes you've just gotta have faith.
I guess some things never change

The fourth time I travelled time
Things started to go wrong
Met myself from the future when I was in the past
It was the version of me that I changed
when I met Jesus
He said that I'd really fucked up the planet
He said World War II never ended
The Beatles never happened
The synthesiser, the drum machine
and the laptop weren't invented
The only place techno now exists is
in your memory and imagination
We need to bring everyone back, reset civilisation
I said but how?
He said "you are exactly where you want to be"
You don't need to go back in time and change history

If you really wanted to be a scuba diver
then you'd have a tank on your back
and you'd be underwater
If you really wanted to be a doctor
then you would have tried harder in 4th year
If you really wanted to be married
then you would have popped the question
If you wanted to be sober
you would have stopped drinking
If you want to know where you came from
you would have asked your parents
If you really wanted to be a poet then
you'd be reading a story about time travel
to a room full of your peers
Now you need to travel time again
Explain the plan to me in the past so I can tell you
Then round up all the versions of us
Trick them so they kill themselves
Do you think you can handle that?
I said Hell Yes
You've already seen how that ended at the start

But the last time I travelled time
I never made any changes
I just went to the very end of civilisation
Saw how we reacted
when the sun swallowed us up as it ended

Took a while to find us
Cause we'd been living on Mars
for the last thousand years
Didn't talk to anyone,
didn't look up my great, great, great
to the power of a thousand grandson
Didn't go to any gigs, even though
the rolling stones where still touring
Doing one last reunion to the population
of the moon
Just wanted to remind myself
how small I really am
We're just a tiny blue dot
on a big black map
Everyone you've ever loved, known or hated
Every war, every death, every fresh newborn baby
Is just half a pixel on the screen that is this universe
Cause no matter what you see
you'll always need more proof
The entire works of
William Shakespeare can fit in one fucking ebook
You've just got to believe what your doing is good
I love you man and I know you've travelled a long way
But sometimes
You've just gotta have faith.

ROBINSON
Brian Johnstone

PROSPECTS FOR ROBINSON

I
There is a bridge some miles from the city
known to all,
Robinson amongst them.

Rush hour
and Robinson has parked his convertible
in the shadow of one of the towers.

He is observed
walking with uncharacteristic haste
towards the western footway.

It is getting late.
The light is dimming fast.

II
Robinson passes several strollers.
His agitation is remarked upon.

He is heard to mutter
"Sunday, at five?"
seemingly addressing no-one.

This time determination does not desert him.
Robinson hits the water
at 5.01.
Its depths swallow him,
bubbles passing his ears like music,
presto.

III
On the footway
a Mrs Morse is walking her dog.

She is distracted by thoughts of her lover.
Was that a splash she heard?
"Ah well – those boys...."

The dog, a French poodle,
is pulling at the leash.

Of Robinson, there is
no sign.

IV
Aware of the pressure in his ears,
Robinson is surprised to find himself
conscious.

He remembers breaking the surface
and the acrid taste of the water.
He remembers the lights of the city
distant
and mocking.

He remembers
nothing else.

V
The boat on which he finds himself,
being fastidious,
is not one he would have chosen.

The destination,
Mexico,
some days away.

Robinson spends long hours
staring at the water,
the wake
seeming to have a particular fascination.

He proves oblivious to the weather.
The weather,
equally oblivious, is unchanging.

VI
It is night
and Robinson is alone on deck.
What little light there is is dim and shaded.

The sea is black,
glistening with an oily sheen.
By turns
it attracts and repels.

Somehow
he cannot recover
his previous determination.

Somehow
he does not think he wishes to.

ROBINSON IN MEXICO

I
Robinson had never believed in clichés:
A new life? A new identity?
What did he care?
But here
the anonymity he craved.

Robinson, today,
is no longer Robinson.

No questions.
No need of them. American. Alone.
That is all.

Few words
and a back street bar.

II
Seen in a drug store,
Robinson is observed eyeing the *Luminol*.

Seen in a small arms warehouse,
Robinson is known to have purchased a *.32 Beretta*.
He polishes it nightly.

He is noticed on occasion
walking to the end of the breakwater,
hesitating, walking back.

Whiskey his friend, indecision preys on him.
Time begins to crack.
Inside,
a suddenly garrulous Robinson
makes his mistake.

No-one is surprised at his disappearance.
It had been expected
daily.

III
Robinson, shouldering a canvas grip,
stares at his shoes.
Italian calf,
beaten and losing a sole.

A confused Robinson
fingers a photograph of his first wife,
picks idly
at the dog ears.

Robinson feels he has been here before,
but
cannot quite get a take on it.

The press will come, he feels certain,
asking in bars.

He will evade them. He'd seen to that.

No matter now but
another flight, another jump.

IV
Robinson walks away from it,
wonders where to buy shoe laces on a ship.

A gangplank
and the smokestacks take his gaze.
Ocean Line.
The livery absorbs him with the ship.

Somewhere in a ballroom
a band plays '*There's a Small Hotel*'.

Robinson brushes a fly off his jacket,
notices it is not a fly
but soot.

On the quayside Mexico gets smaller.

Robinson, looking at the waves,
promises them.

ROBINSON AT SEA

I
This is a short trip for Robinson
who welcomes it.
The Atlantic gestures to him.

Speaking to no-one,
Robinson prowls the decks.
He is, as yet
unrecognised.
This is how he hopes it will continue.

Speaking to the steward,
Robinson declares himself
to be
a Mr Blyth.
He is deliberately evasive concerning his plans.

The steward has little time for him.
This is what Robinson prefers.

II
Each morning
Robinson, the man of habit,
smokes a pipe on the aft deck,
his taste for *Sobranie* being the only pleasure left to him.

At twelve sharp
Robinson toys with his luncheon.
His air of abstraction ensures
no companions.

The afternoon Robinson passes alone,
potting billiard balls,
the crack of cue on ball affording some amusement.

On occasion
Robinson is to be observed in the saloon,
a chess problem before him
unresolved.

Cocktail hour
and a reclusive Robinson retreats to his cabin.
He will not be seen at dinner.

III
Where he feels himself to be alone,
isolated in his thoughts,
Robinson is unaware of the speculation he has caused.

His name is on everyone's lips.
Blyth.
Only it is not his name.

The ship hums with theories,
his introspection being an irritant to all.

No-one has got it right
but Robinson is unaware of that.

If any were to approach him,
Robinson would take action. Of that
he is certain.

In the meantime
anonymity fits him like a coat.

IV
The land seems impressive
to Robinson who has been at sea.

Almost without knowing it
the Atlantic,
has flowed beneath his feet.

The waves, thinks Robinson, seem to have been
denied.

A small port.
Robinson looks at the cliffs,
bright and unscaleable in the morning sun.

Taking a pair of sunglasses
from a case in his his breast pocket,
Robinson makes
the briefest of decisions.

He will speak Spanish again,
if only once.

ROBINSON IN RETREAT

I
Two weeks in and the mind is lightening.

Robinson has begun to read again.
He has acquired a small library.
Paperbacks,
army surplus mostly.
Amongst them an ancient *Baedeker*,
maps, a restaurant guide.

Robinson in extremis, planning an excursion,
surprises himself.

II
Slotting a small coin into a telescope,
tourist Robinson
gazes across the straits.

Beyond him,
concrete, a rainwater trap.

A small boy, scientist by nature,
begins an experiment.
Sweating slightly,
Robinson follows the arc of each stone
to where it meets concrete.

Through the lens,
Robinson stares at the trap.
The gully at its foot
seems to him
no bigger than a man's hand.

His money spent,
the lens darkens.

With reflection,
Robinson's time has run out.

III
Booking was always a problem,
requiring fortitude.

Almost too much to bear
for Robinson, the choice of destinations.
He ponders,
savouring the act of pondering, at least.

The agencies welcome him.
It is his money they are after. Robinson knows this.
It does not trouble him at all.

So, Robinson
taking a cruise.

IV
On the waves a boat moves,
cutting the Mediterranean, the middle sea.
And Robinson at the bows,
breathing deeply.

A week gone by, a pattern becomes apparent.

Robinson intently studying the map.
Robinson asleep in a deck chair,
regretting
the missing moments.

At dinner
honoured Robinson seated
at the captain's table, glass in hand.

Days find Robinson at the rail.
He regrets
his lack of camera,
buys a series of cheap postcards
from the on board vendors.

Increasingly,
Robinson finds himself waking refreshed.

There is little to do, thinks Robinson
heading east,
rounding the world.

ROBINSON IN THE AEGEAN

I
Robinson stands at the corner of the rail
in a white linen suit.
He is a long way from home.

Above him,
towering white and crystalline,
the habitations of men
perch
at the peak of day.

A small boat beckons him
shorewards.
Not hesitating Robinson begins his descent.

II
The boat rolls languidly.
Behind him the cruise ship
swings at anchor.

Up into the sky
the cliffs loom grey and purple,
red
in patches.

Distressed
Robinson fears for his stomach.

A scraping and
a throwing of ropes.
Robinson propelled onto the quay.

III
Lying in wait
there are beasts.
Flies
and long ears flicking at the stench.
Cries of
"*Mulari! Mulari!*"
a brevity of intent.

There seems to be no choice.

Robinson mounted in saddle
ready to ascend.

IV
Hooves fumbling on excrement and stone.
The beasts lurching uncomfortably,
taking the bends
wide.

Robinson at the corners
staring down.
His mind crying with possibilities.
Below him
his own bones scattered,
the flesh that troubled him
dispersed.

Robinson clutching at his panama,
holding on.

V
Stair 500.
Dismounted Robinson is alone.
A small crowd surrounds him.
They do not see him
but chatter idly, ignoring his presence.

Robinson looking back over the edge,
staggers slightly.

From his pocket
he takes a monogrammed handkerchief.
Silk, he believes.

VI
The air is powdered with warmth.
Spring
at least
he thinks so.
This is how he remembers it.

Mopping his brow
Robinson turns to the final ascent.

The houses above him glow pink.
Over his shoulder

the sun
begins to set.

ROBINSON REMAINS

I
The day breaks.
Robinson studies the first rays of the sun
illuminating the morning.

A wall of brick and stucco,
marble flagstones outlined in white
and below him
a beach.

A few steps
and with them he is at the edge of the terrace.

The clean air of the south.
Robinson inhales with satisfaction,
filling his lungs.
Around him the brightness becomes the day.

This is what Robinson calls home.
It, in turn, calls him
Robinson.

II
A small boat
bobs by the harbour wall.
It is a small boat. It is nothing
remarkable.

Robinson watches it strain at its moorings,
pull against the swell.
For the meantime
he is still.
He is not conscious of anything
other than observing.

Floating across the bay
a line of buoys indicates his route of escape.

Steamers call
weekly.
Robinson has ceased to notice
the days of their departure.

III
A cry from the houses:
"*Éla*! Robinson!"
His coffee awaits him.
A *metrio* and some ice cold water

With his free hand
Robinson wipes the condensation from the glass, lights
the first cigarette of the day.

He is smoking less, Robinson notices,
writing more.

No-one remarks upon the notebook
he is observed to use,
nor upon the pen he perpetually carries.

This is the purpose of Robinson,
his function.
Ideas interest him.

IV
In the *kafenío*
it is a day like any other.
Robinson studies the scene for clues.

Eyeing the battered piano,
he wonders if he should think of playing again.

Noting the pictures on the walls,
crude in execution,
he imagines improvements to the line,
the composition.

The women chatter.
It has become apparent to Robinson
that they regard him as part of the scenery.
"*Katálaves? Katálaves?*"
they ask repeatedly,
convinced they are getting through.

A puzzled Robinson
tries to understand,
picks up a few nouns: place names, animals.

This is not Spanish.
He will have to work harder.

after the poems of Weldon Kees

VOICES AFTER A TSUNAMI
Emma Lee

The Tohoku Pacific Earthquake (scale 9) and Tsunami hit Japan on 11 March 2011.

1. Coastal

A handshake's worth of stress
caused an earthquake, and triggered a tsunami;
as if a giant bucket of waste water,
left after washing traffic film from a car,
had been knocked over,
sweeping model towns through the garden until
momentum stalls,
it seeps into the ground and people sink into stasis.

2. Shinjuku railway station

I stood on a platform on top of a giant spring, legs braced.
Thought it was a transport bump, but the swaying didn't
stop, just slowed down.
I headed for a wall, my mental earthquake plan in place.
Limbs ached, head span, felt sick.
It passed – don't know how long – and I left to be hit by
the wave of media images.
But still calm, still shaking, still calm.

3. Sendai

I urge everyone to keep alert,
buildings are busted up,
massive billboards about to fall.
Ground still shaking.
People together for warmth.
I can't go home. My house is trashed.
Can't see anything except car lights.
School packed with refugees.
People seemed in high spirits,
a lot of sad faces though.
It's hard to sleep.

4. A Rare Space off Tarmac

A woman sits on a rare space off tarmac,
her boots taken off to allow her feet to breathe
in the smog and smoke-heavy air.
Burnt skeletons of buildings smashed together
 in the waves, coloured by an occasional book
or picture, edges softened by torn bedding and blinds.
She has stopped searching.
Her face contorts.

5. Minamisoma Miracle
(Hiromitsu Shinkawa)

I turned back to collect something.
I can't recall what it was.
To an observer it seems stupid

but it saved my life.
I turned back and what I wanted
to collect has gone.

I don't remember…
I held my breath, closed my eyes,
grabbed something.

Found myself floating, holding my roof.
All that's left.
I clung.

The ocean so flat, so grey,
only passing shattered wood
that used to be homes.

I clung.
I was told it was two days
and I was a miracle.

6. Rikuzentakata, Iwate Prefecture

"I will never forget this for the rest of my life,
and I think it is important that I do not forget this."
(anonymous medical team member)

Where a body is found, the rescue workers tie a red flag
 and offer a prayer.
There are too many flags to count.

Uncooked rice and melted snow
cause gastro-enteritis. When I draw blood, it's black and
thick. Supplies are "on the way."

A week on, the radio announces death tolls.
A newborn cries. A siren signals
a moment's silence at the time the earthquake struck.

A boy reading a book tells me
there's a cloth of time he dreams he could wrap around
the city and take it back to before.

"Are you in love?" a girl asks.
I tell her he has a beard. "Like Santa Claus?
I wonder if he will come next winter.

"My house is gone now.
He will still stop, won't he?
I want my house and my mummy."

We made a footbath, heated with fires
and invited evacuees. "We're pretty much family,"
an old man wipes his face.

In contrast to the mountains of rubble
and muddy ground, the stars are always beautiful against
the black sky every night.

7. The Fukushima Fifty
A skeleton crew who worked in 15 minute shifts.
The World Health Organisation's limit for maximum
exposure to radiation is 500 milliseiverts. At Fukushima,
the tsunami disabled the generators that powered the
cooling systems.

Zircaloy-clad fuel rods
heated and reacted with steam,
oxidising the alloy,
releasing hydrogen.
Failure of the vents
triggered explosions.

Safety Manual didn't cover
working standing in water,
didn't have protective boots,
radiation seeped through.

Want to get the job done.
TEPCO offering higher pay
for those willing to risk
short high level exposure.
It's tempting.

Escaped sickness,
but cancer takes decades
doesn't it?

8. Vapour Trails

The Prime Minister ate cherries for the TV cameras but
my wife triple-checks the source of our vegetables.

The topsoil in the school playground was buried and
replaced. I still keep our children inside.

We boil all our water. I watch the steam as it cools.
If only radiation could be seen as easily.

9. Sunflowers

I'm wading through mud,
planting sunflower seeds:
they suck up caesium radionuclides.
Like everything now, it takes ages.

"You can't touch the ground.
You can't go into the river.
My childhood wasn't like that,
why should my child's be?
I will never return.
I'm not sure if my husband
and I will live together again."

I see small shoots.
Maybe, maybe they will grow.

"I have to work.
I have to eat.
Investigators collect data,
but we don't get information.
I'm tired of worrying."

I can't believe how big
my sunflowers have grown:
shame they will have to be burnt.

REVENANT
Sarah Lawson

The darkness enclosed us, late as it was,
the summer dusk coming down before nine.
Through the trees overhead the Milky Way spilled,
glittered among the persimmons and maples.
Lightning bugs flashed their corn-kernel taillights,
leaving a trail of dots in the night.
Grown-ups sat on the porch smoking their cigarettes, red
dots in the darkness. The evening sank into night
as they talked on the porch and Charlie's laugh
sometimes rang out over the voices of
Bernice and my mother.
                                        The evening was perfect for
hide-and-go-seek. The tree trunks and bushes were
blacker than darkness;
darker than night in the sloping front yard.
We played in the gathering dusk my brother and I,
and the three older boys who belonged to the house.
The house would have given a glow from the windows.
Indoors a light somewhere still burned, perhaps
in the hallway or in the front room, but out in the yard
it was fireflies and stars, the moon perched in the trees,
and the glow from our parents' Camels and Raleighs.

Now looking back on that scene from my childhood,
my thoughts are with those on the porch and their talk.
The subject was grave, I know, and surmise
that it concerned money and bills and a recent divorce.
How carefree we were, playing hide-and-go-seek

in the dark and catching some fireflies to put in a jar
(except that we never collected enough
for the lamp of continuous light
that folklore assured us was easily made).

A night in July, the darkness so thick
it could catch in your hair, we caught lightning bugs;
adults on the porch, making grown-up red dots
that glowed and then faded,
our parents sat in the darkening
twilight in the heat of Midwestern July–
a porch of a farmhouse, with the smell of hay in the air–
hay and mown grass and cornfields that baked in the heat
of the day,
cornfields where at night you can hear the corn grow–
so they say.

We play our games in the gathering dusk,
But what are they saying there on the porch?
That is the reason we came here today,
whatever they're saying. It wasn't because
we wanted to play in the cool of the evening.
It wasn't because we wanted to romp with the dog
or catch fireflies.
                    The talk is in earnest, about jobs,
getting advice, kicking around
some ideas. What to do next? Which way to turn?
The children of course…the job's not ideal,
but the hours… but then, whereas… however… although…
but I heard none of that, no, nothing at all,
because I was about six and had no idea
what grown-ups discussed in the cool of the evening

seated on the veranda of the old farmhouse
the smell of the hay barn around us, perfuming
the night. I romped with the dog and hid in the lilacs.
"Bumblebee, bumblebee, all come in free!"

The dog gets excited and barks, he crouches,
his rump in the air, ready to chase us, as soon as he sees
what we're going to do next – he wants to join in,
our big furry playmate!
Our parents are probably sharing an ashtray.
They talk on the porch about parent type things –
things we can't understand,
about money and taxes and work,
or maybe some gossip: those people who just
moved to town – did they buy that old house
on Mulberry Street?

If I didn't hear then, it's no clearer now,
although oddly enough, I understand more
of what might have been said.
Does one voice betray worry, a concern for the future?
Does someone go back in the house for a paper
and pencil to work out some figures?

They heard our shouts and our laughter, they knew
we were safe and playing nearby. We were part
of the planning (whatever it was),
oblivious as we were to it all.
Perhaps they were glad we knew nothing of what
they were talking about. Childhood is a place
where you don't have to know what worries adults.

The dots on the porch grew dimmer and faded,
one after the other. Darkness in summer
is past a child's bedtime. I slept in the back seat
and had to be carried into the house.
We drove back to town, the windows all open,
and the sharp smell of goldenrod blew through the car.
Grasshoppers and crickets chirped in the fence rows;
the moon was already a dime in the sky.
Our headlights caught rabbits and swarms of night insects;
a June bug smashed into our windshield,
an acorn with wings.

                         I remember that night
because there were several, and what I remember
is a version of all of them merged into one.
What I remember includes certain things
I didn't know then, so is it a memory
or is it time travel back to watch people who now
are my juniors by a good margin?
I watch us all – the children we were, the grass cooling off
enough to form dew, the air cobwebby with dark,
the scent of fresh hay,
and the adults sitting out on the porch,
thoughtful and serious in ways that we couldn't imagine,
and now my revisiting the scene in a way
that they would find startling; spying on the past
as though saying to them – now out of hearing
even more than we children were then – well done,
if anything failed to work out
it wasn't your fault;
you made good decisions;
your judgements were sound.
What else could you do? I wish you could know –
could have suspected on those warm nights –

that I would remember it all these years later,
would look back and approve, making surmises,
combining the child and the later adult,
standing beside you on the shadowy porch
in the fumes of the Camels and Raleighs,
not quite overhearing, but knowing enough.

I can almost sit listening to their porch conversation:
We're all drinking coffee with cigarettes after;
The children are whooping and running under the trees;
We talk about papers that have to be signed,
Contracts, agreements, a phone call to make.
The dilemma is stated; Bernice has a question.
There are minor dilemmas that stem from the main one.
Charles invariably has an opinion,
and now he explains what needs to be done,
but drawbacks develop that he hadn't thought of,
and so the discussion continues.

My mother is thoughtful; she weighs the suggestions;
she values their insight; she tamps down tobacco
against the nail of her thumb; there's the flare of a match.
She has nearly made up her mind. She'll decide
the next day after mulling it over some more.
Soon she must leave and get the children to bed.
They say their good-byes and she picks her way
to the car, calling to us, (one last wisecrack
from Charles); then reversing the Buick
by the gate to the barn and driving back out
to the road, the car crunching on gravel
all the way to the paved county road,
country smells filling the car, the warm earthy smell
of the fields. In the distance somebody's dog

has encountered a skunk, the pungency drifts
across the dark night and the dense fields of corn.
The headlights pick up the road back to town
and the air is dusty with insects.

Now the air is also dusty with time.
The old Buick was scrapped decades ago;
those grown-ups who lately sat on the porch
are dead and that porch belongs to somebody else.
They still sit in my memory, dots on the porch
in the gloaming with bats flitting high between trees,
fluttering like scraps of burnt paper.
Those decisions that didn't concern me
of course concerned me, even if I didn't know
what they were. So the road unrolled in the lights
continues forever; the summer nights
out where they said you could hear the corn grow
are fixed in a place where nothing much changes,
but events still live in the round
so that you can go back and examine them secretly,
still out of earshot but sharing those nights
of unresolved talk and games never finished.
Poised in uncertainty sixty and more
years in the past, they live for as long
as I can remember being a child of six
in the summer where tangible darkness
held the flashing of fireflies, the scent of fresh hay.

RHYTHMS
Adrienne Silcock

No   she says   no
how there is rhythm to everything   a nightjar piping
          someone told her it was electronic peeping
     a device against mosquitoes
                              a device built to destroy
as if nature could not invent regular rhythm
needs of mankind always centred
                         Need

     No
the dull rhythm of traffic   swish   swish
sounds somehow different at night   enhanced
          according to
Stephen Hawking, there is
                         scientific basis for this
No
     even rise and pitch of people from the village
spilling from a dinner party   laughter and voices
waves towering and rolling forward on to the accepting
                         sand
Please   I am exhausted
too tired to accede   too tired to fight
     you like it really
No   not tonight
     He has never done this before
                    forced his rhythm upon her
     Afterwards she lies listening
to the lift and fade of his breath

lift and fade   lift and fade
   a complacent rumbling through his airways
      Next day
      they sit side by side on towels on the sand
His and Hers
                        she is sitting on the one embroidered His
in cobalt thread   the same colour as the sky
                  as piercing as a stare
   the heat trenchant   unrelenting
like being under a magnifying glass
                              not even a sigh from the sea
as if it is holding its breath
   she can't understand
   waves whip up   bark like a frightened dog at smooth
      curve of sand separating Mediterranean and pine forest
         they pitch forward but stay in the same place
   it doesn't do to show your fear

                                 they bark
   ready to turn tail from the muscle of the land
the dog runs from her mind   thinks
      this island is a beating heart   it understands
            but he does not
      along the coast she can see the mountains
or rather
         where the mountains would be, were it not for
the glowering cloud hanging heavy on the island's
bony shoulders   like an outsized overcoat
      he follows the line of her vision from the cobalt
   gaze and the stifling heat to the foreboding cloud
      on average, he jokes, *the weather is just right*
she is not in the mood for jokes   or averages
it was good last night
she can see the need for reassurance in his eyes

84

a fleck of what may be guilt
she rises to her feet and plunges into the sea
fights through tower and plummet of water
swims beyond where the waves are breaking
lifts and drops with the rhythm of the ocean
seeks out the ocean floor with her feet
allows them to settle into the soft sand bed
surfaces
turns towards the pointillist cloud
here, over centuries, there have been rhythms
invaders
landing with the tide right here on this very spot
maybe
carving roads up into the snowy granite mountains
hunter-gatherers   Greeks driven from Greece
Romans   Vandals Goths Byzantines
Langobards   Moors   Genoese   French   Nazis
and now
the head-banded Moor   everywhere
on flags towels chinaware posters key-rings tea-trays
once the figure of a woman
eclipsed like a new moon by a clear-eyed man
a rhythm of invaders in search of...
in search of...
land   wealth   sustenance   power
pouring their own mores over the island
like olive oil over bread
you cannot remove it
invaders
beating tracks through tangle of oak, Laricio
pine, chestnut
over corrie and ridge, ravine and crashing river of
snowmelt

ransacking hidden villages
to take what they considered theirs
people
swerving their members into women like swords
binding their arms　　　　　　carrying them away
loading them on to their ships
like sheaves of wheat to be sold at market
establishing a slave trade-route rhythm
returning　　　　　returning　　　　returning
like the tide and the moonlight
She allows the waves to wash her
to bowl her back to the shoreline
like driftwood　　weed　　　　　　a single leaf
he watches　　　still sitting
knees drawn up to his chest
arms folded across the top of them
she approaches　　　　　　laughing now
dripping water　　　　skin glistening
he smiles
I will run, she thinks　　　back to the city
slip away amongst the crowds
cast off my shackles
I love you he says
No　　　you do not　　　　　no　　no

BEWCASTLE POINT-TO-POINT
Geraldine Green

I
Tap house
bath house
Romano-Celtic
Goddess
Coventina
you were here first

your feet planted
firmly at this trough
on this earth

dripping tap
world of water
let me enter.

II
The tree of life and land
leaves
the staring
Alpaca behind

III
Long road leads north
out of England
west the Way of the Sun.

Old barn
god of many winters
corrugated, louvred
receptacle for all that is
rubbish and holy.

a red tractor approaches
now I must move.

IV
If I turn
180 degrees
if I turn even 90
if I let…
the wind
bows before me

V
a sheep has croup

clouds hang from telegraph wires
so much washing!

Beyond the horizon Rome
beyond the horizon clouds
beyond the horizon home

who pegged these clouds to the sky?

VI
A stand of fir trees
puncture the blue

pale stars tear the fabric of clouds

VII
My legs warm
in the sun

hens chuckling.
Meadow and dung.
Rough lichened stone

fells
fold
one
into
the other

VII
Alpacas
like Romans
and apples
and me
strangers here,
belong nowhere.

Pretty Alpaca face!
what are you watching?

IX
Here's a wall
around the castle.
a moat
dry and empty

filled with munching and daisies.
We swing by in a 12-pointed circle
spinning here on earth in this place
of pilgrims.

X
Soon I'll be at the bull gate.
A midge lands on the page
pepper-speck on paper.

XI
One sits by the gate.
One stares at the castle.
One says, ok,
next please, move on.

We shuffle our way
human water meandering
round the moat

inside out and ducks
outside in and sheep.

Scotland invades in a thistle
It accompanies me on my walk.

XII
Bewcastle stones eat sky
rotten stone molars
bite history and air

The Alpaca stares.
Sky circles.
News of war
electrifies
…Legions
Reivers
Wounded Knee
Ghandi
ash clouds
Euro crash…

news buzzes over us

A blind lamb
hunkers down
under the sun
wind blows cold.
This ruin leans south west
Home is behind me
in front, clover.

Keep off!
a sign
at the top
of the slope
tells us
follow lower route
beside moat

cattle,
small black
medium red
large white
hefted here
on no-man's land.

On the fell
to the south
one house
stops
its mouth
others stare
wide-eyed

XIII
Corvus Raven
Crow Morrigan
Two black feathers.

Dribble falls from the bonny calf's nose
ruler-straight back, young bullock.

Everything here watches

All eyes on Rome.
All eyes on Reivers.
All eyes on us, now.

XIV
A yellow tractor tumbles
down the fellside.

XV
Still I'm observed:
day's eye
hidden flange of moon

Alpaca shakes itself free
of midges
of air
of sun
and wind
and strangers.

Irritation in
its calendar of Peruvian genes.

XVI
Thistle.

XVII
Feet trample Fat Hen.

More thistles
Inside the circle
sunlight.

A crack in the wall.
shit streaked.
Wall of stone.
Wall of lichen.
Wall of blood,
wall
of boiling oil.

This is a country of gates and walls
these debatable lands, batable ground
threap lands lying between kingdoms
to which do you belong?

News speaks to me from ochre lichen.

XVIII
In a small byre wall a half-door, half open.

IXX
the weathervane on Saint Cuthbert's is handsome
but not the church.

Land of church and gates.
Land of fells and walls.
Land of boundaried horizons.

Tell me
what's over there
that I just can't see?

XX
The crack.
The falling.
The tumble.
The warring.
The cross.
What holds?

I stumble.

XXI
Blind church
I don't
like you.

Hunchbacked.
Mouthed, mealied
mock-humble.
Walled in yews.
Firs, sycamores.

Escape!
God's sake
you know
you want to.

Swallows click clack
chitter
whirr
their gossip
over telegraph wires

XXII
the wind prophesies
strands of hair
plait my mouth

A gap
in the wall
like me, will open.

XXIII
You're not wholly black
you straight-backed cattle
the sun through your ears
turns them to autumn

and where are your morning calves?
I see. One's a shadow.

Tipping fell.
Pilgrim sky.
Sunlight unpicks mortar
from the clouds.

At the gate
dripping
an old
iron tap
offers water
time ripples

I dip in
My hands
smell earth
cupped palms to face
nose, mouth

blue sky bleeds into yellow sun
crazed cracked cockerel calls me

O! the miracle of bellowing!

XXIV
My breathing.
His walking.
Her questions.
Swallows' answers.

Red tractor
colour of
solid motion.

Under clovered earth
a small purple flame
I enter its iris, searching.

The crack
the cross
the tumble

my back is wall
my legs are road
this track around
the empty moat
a pilgrimage.

'I' no longer holds good

I no longer
hold on
to anything

I'm caught in this wide tumbrel of sky.

Tonight, when I look at the stars
will I hear the gossip of swallows
 spark and crackle?

XXV
Ridged moat
a fingernail

of time, scraping
lichen and itches
scratches our unknown.

If I lie down.
If I lie, face close
to the earth
face down I mean, nose to ground
listening

will I hear legions breathing?
Or will I hear my own shadow
calling me home?

XXVI
door stands half open
before me

I complete the circle.

XXVII
This telegraph pole
holds a crown of thorns.

Would it help
to be part of
the speckled hens'
shit smelling henhouse?

XXVIII
Almost home.

XXIX
Kissing gate
Opens.
Behind me
the ruin
the moat
Alpaca
Romans
Bath house
Trough of
Coventina.

And now I'm unsure
Have I circled this place
or been circled?

A tree ring of time
dizzy with sky.

Light opens a fraction.
Gate closes
Sky circles.

I settle down to roost
sun-warmed

gate opens
gate closes
tap continues
dripping
stone lintels hold sway here
water tumbles into concentrics

the tap's pipe lagged
with frayed white plastic
a farmer's feed sack
not gone to waste.

The lamb with no eyes
beh's for its flock,
crouches down
kneels, blind pilgrim
front legs tucked under
back legs follow

looks up
sniffs diesel
from the tourist's coach
– just leaving
sniffs air
swallows' crackle
with fire.

The twenty-first century leaves

Spadeadam's satellites
look on unseen.

THE BLACK LIGHT ENGINEER
p. a. morbid

The Black Light Engineer I.

 slowly from the east or at least what I think of as the East
for there is no direction in the confines of this limitless void Softly
    In some hour of declension a lessening of shade

    Movement
   (ripples of time)   Nothing so soft as the fall of a key
(hurtling)   Through space falling Landing noiselessly

    Like a brittle arch this silence   this breaking up of the
tense
inner light   Nothing moves? I see broken clock insides
            (inside my head)

Time-less instance of unrecorded past. Behind me –
Time: a discontinued Expanse of remorse

          Memories pile up
   & bring me nothing but pain

   Something to weigh me down/
   Something to hold.   Again. ---- the slow ache of the
Aeons; the light they emit   Intolerably bright
       the rhythm of the stars random
senseless.   He turns to leave. But where can he go?

This boundless space is empty of movement.

102

A chill. entering through the brain   and fingers.

                                        Ice thickens
    the pain blackens and becomes something other than itself
Slowly time
    Is falling   Falling asleep...

Keep the emptiness I have in the stomach   Exasperated he chokes
                                                back his tongue
    a useless gesture of   ingratitude   And Defiance

Once these arms lay locked in another's
                    Now only the gaseous wastes occupy his bed

        The night outside – so deep in its arching, spreading form
that the Trumpet-Call to the End goes by unnoticed so loud is
the Silence

If at Night   (what light other than this darkness?)
If at the remembrance of dawns light broken
                                    he remembers his Life
                    (the subtle energies play)

Then what gift for the closing years?
what gift of forgetfulness will ever fill that Chasm?

Sense is senseless   It evades so many unanswered questions

        – Questions –

        Unnamed lest they be answered & then what?

The Black Light Engineer II.

                                        Dimly the Radio signals fade.

Fade into Nothing
It is nothing to fear
            Fear lest the hands grip into claws and the fear chokes
                        the fear strangles
    There is no point of light against the immensity of this blackness.
    If you press your hand to my head you will feel there the roaring
the total stupidity of the physical universe

                                        Known/Unknown

how it all remains? So savage along its blunted edges
                                    no more
                                    the raging torrent of life
                                    of newly-created
                                    SUNS

Here where no stars breed   I feel the weight of all the dead stars

I feel. --- yet feeling is not enough   it is the turn of the
universe

                                    This puts a strain on my neck.
                                    On my arms
                                    And on the backs of my arms
You sing: I sing the song of universal Inertia

No more strain.   No more fighting.   No more anything.
Slowly it envelops

---- EVERYTHING ----

No more.   Soft lullaby of dying stars.

No more.   The coasting   The rising   falling equilibrium

I don't tell her where to go It is a deep climb.

Up from this hell there is no escape from ----

it comes undone in my hands ---- these hands reach out

something so slow --- slower than ice forming

Even fear has departed me:
I stand clear of the stars & the cold stellar winds rock me to sleep
in my bed

Hush!   I find an incline that is broader than deep.
So deep I   Cannot take it.

It moves towards some sickle town

(no moon in the sky)

In this place of shadows I feel, that last soft touch   I feel your heart
as it beats out my name

You are dead   You are not dead
You are dead

He sees her as an eternity   doomed to repetition.

All the brown stars, pointless
in their brief, idle turning. A yawn   a gaping hole

moves out from his heart & opens

something senseless

something hidden
hidden
or despised

an empty cradle
easy as passing through
Through the brain
of an eagle

Climbing upwards with ever-faltering steps
                he moves his arms
wide against the thickening blanket of stillborn stars

Where is she? that warm darkness?
                    He wishes for an angel a smothering hand

    Yet still she won't come

    low rumble of distant skies   red-shift:
departing stars – caught on the surface of my mouth
                                        the lips
tingle
                        Anticipatory light
an all pervading Dullness   an Unbreachable gap

                            hollowed out or
            Cast away by uncaring hands   They swell & they die

a veil across his memories
inane laughter
echoes down the years   all time cut into pieces
                        will not bring you closer

The bright lights   departing sweetly O so sweetly
                              a Universe so dissolute.   yet still

from my arteries & veins the blood still Still in the night, flows

& like everything else
it flows away from me
                    Lost
            in some suffering period of dense, stifling light.
                    That breaks up
Into its composite atoms   Spiral-Shapes
                    That deny my experience

     While
     From between my thighs
a long line of diseased eggs   laughing at their
                         own existence

The Solar disc flares in his hands, It burns away his flesh.
                              Flash of the Beginning
     that rupturing Spark that   split the Universe in two In three
The Solar disc dies as he holds it
                    Hard against his breast.
                              It is hard inside there.

There were the Aeons beat endlessly.   There were the Angels speak.
See how your form moves out from me   Elusive   Spreading
                              Darkness all about.

The Angels singing in your wake. Wait!
                         I see you now...

The End is the same as the
Beginning

The horses drown
The horses drown in blackness

And no one will see.

The Black Light Engineer III.

Such sorrow at the passing   all the lines of empty space
                               This life   such life as it is
Remains only in your head

In broken angles of fractured time

                    little by little it unfolds
            enfolding   (engulfing)
                all of the wasted spaces No continuum
    nothing but the fall of ashes

                        LILTING

– A move towards enlightenment   cruel abandonment

                               It loses all shape
                                 All shape is lost
                                    its sharp edges blur
Into one solid mass of light   Black light
                            In a heaven that refuses to bleed
                          Inchoate

Spiralling backwards   till it remains out of sight.
hidden by gas clouds   and choked on ice

        the bright red wound
                            Something definite

            deep inside
                    where
            angels wake

Wait!   I sense something now

                    It gathers
                        to itself   a lull in time?
A broad spatial harmony
                Somehow it comes unstuck: breaking up

            all alone – it comes to you
Suddenly I thought it gone that somehow it wouldn't be there

            a deep menstrual wound that
probing fingers cannot touch   help me

It comes not
to you   Silently you wait   I can hear the singing,
        I call your name though
                            I cannot see you

    the dead stars sleep on in
                some nameless forever
                        sleeping.   never to wake
        the sky just goes on   it's so insane it's stupid

endlessness   never
ending   and all always sleeping
                       I scream against it   but the
night has wings   to take flight and dive at me

        So much time & space to move in.

    I am not the duration   I am a period of infinite regress.
         I ache in huge cyclic movements

                 the Ice giants crouching
       Blocking off the known universe

We thrive in Iceolation: Period   Red Shift   the tears spiralling
   forming pools I cannot drown in
                     Survival means pain
the
proof of my body, my frail Identity
Disgust at this fleshy mass

I hate the silence   It feeds on me
                  on the slow mechanical movement
      of arm and chair   What difference is there?
                The difference I see
   –   Colour and shape   –
                  form pools of experience
           I cannot drown in
I am condemned to Eternal light
        Black-light Engineer on the edge of Oblivion

I long for absolution but what light survives this blackness?

I remain committed to my task

NAVIGATOR

Mid-heofon flight

Alone

NAMING: AD 2006
Alwyn Marriage

i.
Each knew he'd made another friend,
but didn't realise this time it was for life;
in cultivating this relationship,
they'd both dug lasting treasure.

D'you know their faithful dog?

They live
near the kirk
up the hill
from the Firth
of Forth.

There's nothing humdrum, inane
or ordinary about their house:
alive with conversation, argument and laughter;
a winter garden full of candle light,
a summer house that sways between the trees.

D'you know the name of their dog?

Aidan, Douglas, Druminane and Juno,
all spoken, woven in a skein and hidden.
So words and names can be concealed
in sentences that don't relate
to their reality.

ii.
There was a time, not very long ago,
when love like this led only to denial;
those who were joined were rudely torn apart;
a satisfying synthesis like this between the law
and art was then impossible.

That night has passed, new light
has dawned in which we recognise at last
that we should not conceal, apologise or blush,
but celebrate this love that dares to speak its name.

iii.
Taboos have changed, and now
other linguistic limitations
constrain our civil ceremonies;
words and sacred names prohibited,
that otherwise might play a part
in defining and in dedicating
what is done today.

So I will not utter any name
as I call down blessings, pour libations,
burn the sacred flame.

My lips will speak of Plato's Eros;
I'll expound Hindu mythology; and, while
eschewing hymns long sung at football grounds,
I'll add my music to the Song of Songs.

And as appropriate epithalamium
for this commitment, I'll pause to contemplate
l'amor che move il Sole e l'altre stelle.

Confident that Dante can be quoted without blame,
we'll bless this partnership and celebrate
an even greater love that dares to speak its name.

A VISITATION AT THE ABBEY OF BARKING
Judi Sunderland

Let me tell exactly how it was.
It happened in this Abbey, in the years
before Abbess Ethelburga was led out
from the prison of the flesh. The year of plague
when many brother monks, our near neighbours,
were gathered to the company of Heaven.

Our Reverend Mother called us all to prayer to seek
God's guidance; where to dig our graves,
for it was likely some of us would perish, and after Lauds,
the sisters all went out into the brothers' graveyard,
praising God when all at once – at once – let me recall –
– a blinding light from Heaven covered us like a sheet,
but bright as many suns and a sound,
a thousand beating wings thundered in our ears.
To us it seemed the light was searching out our human souls
 and finding every one of us unholy.

And this is where my words are insufficient
but call to mind the witness of Ezekiel – the first chapter.
Then we felt a mighty wind and the vessel in the sky; the ship,
or chariot, hovered like a goshawk, like a portent from
the end of days, or their beginning,
of Nephilim or Seraphim, or Demons;
but in its centre, in a shell of crystal there seemed a Man.
And Brother, now I tremble to say what sinful thing
befell us there.

We bowed down, each of us, and worshipped
and begged the thing for mercy.
Was that blasphemy, my Brother?

If so, I fear my soul has not been shriven.

I will continue. As we lay prostrated
the Being moved, but slowly, hung in glory
west of the Oratory, where its bright beam seemed
 to indicate a place.
And then it rose; into the sky and vanished from our sight.
All of the nuns who dwelt here saw the vision;
Torhtgyth, Edith, Mother Ethelburga.
But now I am the only one still living.
My sisters now lie peaceful in the earth beneath
the place the heavenly creature hallowed.
Please God, and I will not be long to join them.

GRASS WAS TALLER
j.lewis

sheep springs
is clearly in the
    middle of nowhere
not four-corners qualified
or capitol of anything
it boasts only the trading post
a small cafe and
the chapter house mandated
by tribal headquarters
for local...

  in reservation terms
  that would mean something
  between 50 and 100 square miles
  of sand and sagebrush
  interspersed with dry washes
  arroyos that can fill
  and kill in an instant
  when rain on distant mountains
  comes too much too fast and
    finding it cannot seep down
    into the earthy womb that opened for
    the first kachinas and the
    afterbirth of navajo mythology
  flees the hills and rushes dirty red
  down the previously mentioned

dry washes without warning
  across highways
  where dips instead of bridges
  surprise unwary tourists

...meetings and events of grave importance
like the theft of hosteen's saddle
the one his father gave him
 u.s. cavalry insignia
still deeply embossed...

  hosteen recounts again
  how the soldier with the sad eyes
  had no other apology
  after the infamous long walk
  simply took the saddle from his horse
  set it at father's feet
  and rode away bareback
  shoulders slumped with the burden
  of turning warriors into shepherds
  because the telling of the story
  is a vital page in their book of remembering

...which the tribal police duly noted
and will watch for at
the fair at window rock
the rodeo at shiprock
though everyone knows there is little hope
the saddle will be found

while hosteen slowly shakes his head
at the loss of this piece of his past
his face shows no emotion
for that is not the navajo way
instead he talks of days
when the now dry reservation grew green
with grass that reached the stirrups of the saddle
that is gone
the drought that took it all away
days when he could leave things atop his corral
and they would stay
it is not right he says that the honor
of our people has dried up like that grass

I HAVE NO FEET
Bernie Howley

(*Finally, to take a step without feet*, Rumi)

One should stand, poised,
like Athena in all her sculpted wisdom,
serene and steady
atop a skinny stone-hewn plinth,
gazing, unblinking, to the distance
to the landscape, its creatures.
One really should stand poised.

> *But I grip the cliff wall wishing with fervour that
> my fingers ended in suction pads, draw breaths,
> deep breaths which I blow out in noisy exhalations
> while imploring a god I don't believe in to save me.
> I whimper; scrunch shut my eyes. Finger by finger I
> release my grip and feel my way down onto all fours
> and, finally, to undignified cliff-top prostration. Oh,
> Athena, there may be a view, there may be wildlife,
> but I don't bloody-well care.*

One should take wing, lightly,
as a kite lifts heavenward
on thermic cushions,
pinions twitching,
to descend and carve
fat, luxurious spirals through air.
One really should take wing lightly.

Face down on the precipice the cries of my kids ring in my ears, 'You can do it, Mum,' and I wonder why they want me to die. But worse, when my eyes at last agree to open, I spy spectators. Offspring hollering's drawn a crowd... of young Italian studs, ones who throw themselves off these cliffs all day long, for fun, all Peter Pan and cocky. Muttering, I reverse my routine: in tiny incremental shuffles, from prostrate back to all fours to pause, my next move anathema. But the minds eye, having taken on the main optical function, supplies a timely image. I now see myself as an old, plump component of an Allen Jones coffee table... on a cliff top. Pronto, I find the perpendicular and I look... down.

One should evaluate, capture,
in true Arthus-Bertrand fashion
the shoaling fish that iridesce, circling,
lip to tailfin, fish-eye to flank,
to make a million interlocking, silver rings.
One really should evaluate and capture.

I leap. Mid-flight, I pinch shut my nose and hope to withstand any uncomfortable up-rushes so reducing the chance of choking, at least. Bare rock and tufts of greenery flash by. I hover in a time warp. 'What-if' thoughts stream through my head. What if... I hit the fish? Will they die? What if... I hit the rocks? Will I die? What if... my bikini top comes off? I. Will. Die. What if my lungs fill with water? I die if not already dead. What if the shoaling fish eat me? What the

fuck, I'm already dead. I tuck my knees up to stall,
for a futile nano-second, the inevitable discomfort,
my possible demise, my certain embarrassment. The
water hits.

One should streamline on entry,
as does the kingfisher.
Pleated and neatly tucked in,
the paper-plane bird with go-faster,
dive-deeper strip plunges, splashless,
to fishing depth, turns tail
to break the surface once again,
unfurls it folded colours
flashes an orange under-wing
and steals away, beakful with quarry.
One really should streamline on entry.

GRITHSPELL
Math Jones

In eldest days, when Ymir's blood
Was steaming still and stars unsure
Rehearsed their roads, then rode to Thing
The tired gods. Tyr and Odhin,

Moody Æsir, met the Vanir
Under shade of shattered fences –
Etin's eye lash, iron-timbered –
Root up-ripped, rubble now.

Spoke the Thing-God, "Think on this:
Tried we have in trading blows
To quell the other – but quickness leaps
In both our bloods and brooks no victor."

Njord gave answer: "Never would
We see an end to sorry strife,
But that Baleworker take back his spear,
Forego his prize and fight no more."

"You spit, Spear-God, spurn our truce?
Fetch me then my father's cup
To catch that spittle – spare it not!
But drain the dregs of dragons' spite."

Odhin spoke a spell of rage,
In fury forged, flung it over
The gathered hosts, gave them answer:

"Sore it is to fight a war and not to win
And so I spit!
Sore it is to see friends harmed and not avenged.
Sore it is to see a foe do hurt to mine,
To do me wrong,
And not be made to pay and pay
And so I spit! I spit!

"Sore it is to find my blade unsharp and cutting not my foe.
Sore it is to see my foe and spare his life!
Sore it is that so much blood of friends is cast about
And too little,
Far too little,
Of mine enemies let.

"Sore it is that all the worlds and all of Wyrd
Moved not my way, nor to my will,
But let me hang – einherjar –
One, at war, alone and with myself.

"To rid the taste of bile and spew, of spear-iron, I spit.
Of defeat, distrust and shame, I spit.
Of scorn and mockery, I spit.
Fury, sweat and fear, I spit.
Fire, I spit.
Blood, I spit,
And reckless, heedless haste.
I spit derision and indecision,

Grief and hurt, unlooked-for malice,
Ire and bitter betrayal...
Loss, I spit!
And loss again, of love and all-is-well
And all-wise, all-seeing, always right... so too I spit!

"I spit for witnesses to my wrong-doing, left living to
speak against me.
I spit for children's tales and nurses' rhymes which speak
of my defeat.
I spit that no god steered my hand, but mine own.
I spit that Ymir's flesh, though dead, still pulls me down!

"I spit for arms and head
And shoulders, legs and gut aching from the end of
strain.
I spit for the scorn in my Freya's face.
I spit for the skill I gain in parry and strike.
I spit for the hidden mock my foeman has
Within his hall of me and mine.

"For safe return of my sons, I spit.
For home and hall standing,
For harvest and cattle safe,
For hall unburnt,
For the praise of my fathers.

"For I see a doughty warrior, I spit.
For I see my foeman's worth, I spit.
For I could not defeat him,
Nor he, I.

That our efforts were matched
Blade for blade,
Blow for blow,
Blood for blood
And head for head,
Heart for heart,
Mood for mood,
For that I spit
And faith and frith
And for the weary weakness of my arm
And aching lung
And sorrow to my very soul,
My ferth."

So spoke each, so spat each,
With mither and malice.
More than another
Could no wight gather.
More than another could no wight carry:
Bale from the battle,
Bile from the belly.

So spoke each, so spat each,
Till gall was gone and guts were dry.
Ale was brought, brewed by the Vanadis,
Holy in horn – and hostages named.

`Neath the world-tree, the Nornir worked;
Hung their loom with lines of drool
And spittle-threads. The spinsters turned
The glistening gob to golden blood,

To knotted sinew, knitted bone,
Brought from out the brimming cup
A bright-faced man, broad in wisdom:
A canny man, Kvasir hight.

ORION
Simon Brod

A hunter should walk upright
on the skyline, eyes open
to see as far as the stars

in the fearless night,

but here you are upside down
as day drains down from the sky,
with only your legs showing,
a boy diving for trinkets
fiddling blind in the seabed.

You've been holding your breath all day.
The ancients were wrong, you know –
it's at night sight is keenest,
when all the creatures gather
to question the crystal dark.

Dusk ebbs past your chest, your chin,
your eyes. Then you fill your lungs
and leap to your feet. You're in
the big game, clothed in soft breeze
stalking the bear, the black bear,
his gentle paw on raw earth

in the juniper night,

the faithful air tells his path,
brings you musk, dung, warm fur, sweat.
Moving at an easy lope
soundless over the dry earth

in the loose-limbed night,

your blade at your belt,
your net slung on one shoulder, its stone weights
bulking it like a coiled asteroid,
you stretch your ears
towards the rustle of leaves

in the wide-awake night,

the faint scratch of claws on bark.
You crouch, wait, you're motionless,
you use his eyes, his whiskers,

in the birch bole night

listen to his slow breathing,
his beating blood stretch time taut

in the bow-string night,

till you know his next desire.
All at once you release, whirl
your net, it leaps from your hand

like a sudden storm, its stones
slingshot his dense emptiness,
briefly orbit as he roars,
collapsing in on himself

in the star-braced night.

Your blade finds his heart, stops it.
Black pours over the parched earth.

And you think you're nearly home
as the wind rises, circles

in the sibilant night

where the sky is wide open,
but you're not done yet: you must
chase across your father's fields
after the charging bull.
His flanks glisten quicksilver

in the blackthorn night,

eyes flash diamond,
hammer-forged hooves ring like a regiment
on the baked earth, the glassy air
shatters from the wide tips
of his horns rushing towards
the sea's edge as the wind whips

in the diapason night

and the world cracks and rattles.
Looking only to the kill

in the splintering night

you're faster than him, nearly
ready to wrestle him down
when he gives a great snort, turns
to face you for the last time

in the night that rolls out of reach –

then dawn creeps up, takes your sight
and you trip and go flying,
legs high in the fading sky,
head underwater in day,
fingers scrabbling in new-laid sand.

ERIS SPEAKS
Cathy Bryant

I was banned from the wedding
like a disgraced aunt or an ex.
They said I would cause trouble.
This from Zeus,
The multiple rapist.

At bottom I did not really want to be
in another family photograph,
the long shot with everyone smiling
as if they were enjoying it.
But it would have been nice
to have been asked.

How much I was blamed!
Yet all I did was to make an apple
of gold and write on it 'Kallisti'.
Paris should have thrown it
to the sunset or the sea.

Poor Helen got blamed too,
But pretty faces do not launch ships.
Other people
Made war and killed.
There would have been no harm done
if Menelaus had shrugged and said,
"Let them be happy."
If he had known how to grieve.

I am a footnote in the family history,
a lie written up.
Every year or so those who attended
and gossiped, think of me for a moment
and feel uncomfortable.
This is their choice, not my gift.

I wanted to come to the wedding,
and my gift was a golden fruit.
I had planned it to be for the firstborn
of Peleus and Thetis:
a new baby is always the fairest.
I cried when they could not have it.

I would do no direct evil.
I am not a multiple rapist
and I do not make war.
I gave them the chance
to show their true selves.
This is the nature of tragedy,
the consequence of unkindness.

IN RETAIL (XXIII)
Jeremy Dixon

Good morning.
Do you have an advantage card?
And would you like a bag?
Please enter your PIN.

Good morning.
Thank you for waiting.
Do you have an advantage card?
And would you like a bag?
Please enter your PIN.

Good morning.
Thank you for waiting.
No one's answering the bell.
Do you have an advantage card?
And would you like a bag?
Please enter your PIN.

Good morning.
Thank you for waiting.
No one's answering the bell.
They're all at a meeting without me.
Do you have an advantage card?
And would you like a bag?
Please enter your PIN.

Good morning.
Thank you for waiting.
No one's answering the bell.
They're all at a meeting without me.
Seems I'm the only one left in the shop.
Do you have an advantage card?
And would you like a bag?
Please enter your PIN.

Good morning.
Thank you for waiting.
No one's answering the bell.
They're all at a meeting without me.
Seems I'm the only one left in the shop.
I could find myself with a riot on my hands.
Do you have an advantage card?
And would you like a bag?
Please enter your PIN.

Morning.
Thank you for waiting.
No one's answering the bell.
They're all at a party without me.
Seems I'm the only one left in the ship.
I could find myself with a riot on my hands.
Yes, you're right it isn't good enough is it.
Do you have an advantage card?
And would you like a bag?
Please enter your PIN.

Mourning.
Thank you for belling.
No one's answering the weight.
And there's another party without me.
Seems I'm the only one left in the world.
I could find myself with blood on my hands.
Yes, you're right it isn't God enough is it.
You would have to talk to my mother.
Have you taken the advantage?
And do you need a nosebag?
Please enter your PAIN.

FAITH IN A TIME OF DOUBLE-DIP RECESSIONS.
Inua Ellams

– for those who pray for money.

Once in the blue moon of my prayers,
I rise, brush the dust off my knees and
imagine the answering angel hears me
as Tiger Woods might sense a far hole:
such fields of folks, of distance to cover
and one stroke to get it right. The angel,

he floats down and with the featherest
of touches taps a bus driver's shoulder
vanishing in a puff of something warm
that smells like home. She turns, sniffs.
A sudden longing hits her gut. The bus
stalls for ten short seconds but it's long
enough for Ahmed to sulk off, hail a taxi,
ask the chatty driver politely to shut up
and drive. Down the road he accelerates
Got to get this bastard off my backseat
he thinks, narrowly missing Mrs Smith
who startles her latte across her blouse,
spews the foulest words. A school girl
passing taps her teacher with That's it!

Daddy used those words! Father calls,
cancels his afternoon mistress to meet
his daughter's teacher for a serious talk
and the angel grips his clipboard, ticks
the box for [ ] Sin Additionally Averted
as he catalogues the toppling dominoes
of his handiwork: that's us. Coiling out
across the city, the magnificent dance
of chance and chaos that few revel in,
many hate, some believe to be ordered
only when desperate, whispering Help,
intense, needing, as I, of money, love
or strength to break a door as a burglar
might when the alarm goes off and old
Miss Williams, arms laden with bin bags
outside the Job Centre where she works,
searches for keys, misses a five pound
note leak from her purse. It falls slow
as feathers, holy as answered prayers
to land among bags of reference letters,
CVs, job applications and exam results:
these littered like discarded dreams of
a generation; a new bag placed on top.

I imagine the angel planned all this, felt
I would step out empty handed, save a
couple pennies tinkling like false gods.
His left wing kinda twitched and he saw

I would come along, head bowed, feet
scuffing concrete, kick one plastic bag
swollen with rain, glimpse the five pound
note I scoop into the emptiness that is
my wallet, lift my voice past skyscrapers,
stars glittering with the mysterious ways
it's said he works in, on, past the angels
to finally thank God.

ON THE HUNT WITH MR ACTAEON
Jill Sharp

So it's me and Percy in the Boxster, lid back, loving
the hiss of our fat tyres flattening her gravel.
When she put GSOH she wasn't kidding:
stucco and naked statues on every wall; a flight
of Portland steps to the gilt-edged door.

I can't have Percy bothering the corgis
so I tie him up outside on a generous lead
beside a drinking trough. He isn't pleased – goes
hangdog on me – but what's a red-blooded chap to do
when he needs a bit of amorous interaction?

Some flunkey lets me in, saying she'll be down soon;
invites me to look around (though I must respect
her private quarters). This woman's got to be Lady
Something-or-other, judging by all these cases
stuffed with taxidermy, these antlered halls.

After a draughty corridor of nymphs, I'm desperate
for the bathroom. Painting's not my thing. I sneak
upstairs, try a few doors ... Relief! I've seen a bath
large as a lido, mountains of bling, but nothing
you'd call 'private', until the second floor...

...and this half-open door, through which a gentle murmur
draws me achingly near. She lets the long robe fall, settles
onto a chair, her flesh aglow from bathing, though to me –
crazy from sudden revelation and dark fantasy –
it bears the expert stroke of a huntsman's whip.

Lips forming a 'because I'm worth it' smile, she basks
beneath the touch of a masseuse as her golden hair
is heaped in braided coils, her long nails painted.
Into the silence, heartbeats, the swift rasp of breath.
All actions cease. Her eyes lock onto mine.

She's responding to my gaze of wild desire
with such Olympian disdain and cruelty
I gasp and flee, hurtle downstairs, dislodging
tapestries and busts, my brow leaden, splitting
like time-lapse shoots have come rioting out.

I reach the portal, hot, hirsute, balancing
on all fours. Now Percy clocks me, leaps to his feet
snarling like Cerberus. Foam slobbers from his jaws
as he surges forward snapping the leash, rushing me
like I'm a bitch on heat – or dead meat...

I WENT TO THE MARKET AND I BOUGHT…
Anne Macaulay

…an avocado –
plump, shiny green outside and knife yielding, soft and buttery within

… a butterknife –
ivory effect handle, blade more for spreading than cutting

… a candlestick –
a centrepiece for blushing glow

…a damask cloth –
white and starched a canvas for the feast

…an envelope –
thick creamy paper, enfolding just words of love

…freesias –
frail yellow and white, scent gently filling a room for two

…glasses –
for filling, fizzing, clinking, sipping

…a handkerchief –
lace edged with a bluebell embroidered in the corner

... ink –
in a squat bottle, purply blue, the colour of lovelorn,

... a jug –
elegant glass etched with a swirl for water to offset the wine

...a kimono –
cream silk with black edging to wear before and after undress,

...a locket –
to hold a picture or lock of someone's hair,

... meats –
to grill on skewers and glisten on the dish

... napkins –
neatly folded to gently dab on lips and chin

...oranges –
round and smiling to float in slices in caramel or freshly squeeze
if breakfast comes

... Parma Violets –
in a tiny tin for sweet scenting lips and breath

… a quill –
to dip carefully in the ink and scratch a trembling declaration
without blotting

… rice –
the kind that is thrown at weddings, and will cook fluffy and
white for dinner

… a scarf –
cream georgette to lay over my shoulders

… Turkish Delight –
rose, lemon and pistachio cubes, in a cloud of icing sugar

… a ukelele –
to strum as we harmonise.

… vanilla icecream –
to marry with sweet oranges and melt with each bite

… wine –
light hearted Prosecco then spicy red Malbec to follow.

… XO Cognac –
to pour in a warmed balloon glass and swirl in cupped hands
before sipping as we face each other

… yellow ribbons –
 to tie in my hair, and on the tree.

I went to the market and I bought...

... an avocado, a butterknife, a candlestick, a damask cloth, an
envelope, freesias, glasses, a handkerchief, ink, a jug, a kimono,
a locket, meats, napkins, oranges, Parma Violets, a quill, rice, a
scarf, Turkish Delight, a ukelele, vanilla icecream, wine,
XO Cognac, yellow ribbons

and finally a zephyr –
it seemed a bargain price but it blew away my basket, everything
                tumbling and
                        floating
                                out of my reach,
                                        my view,
                                                my ken.

THE BROKEN THREAD
Robin Winckel-Mellish

The Khoisan woman wakes,
buttocks slack and shrunk,
skin loose, brittle as burned grass.
She rubs eyes, looks around,
remembers who she was,
asleep for ages, wearied by dreams,
she begins to rise.
Was she dead and now returned to earth?
Her hair outlined in the clouds
she throws a stone to the wind
to see what it will tell –
it becomes a bird and flies away.
A strange new place she thinks,
the land is dry, her tongue is dry,
makes quick excited clicks.

The low brown skyline has scattered
hollow spines of bristled earth,
porcupine twigs poke the sky,
rattle in the wind, a straggle
of white tree limbs, bleached
old bones glint in silence,
the earth hard, dark veined, as if
jutting through aged flesh.

Has the land become the moon? the Khoisan woman
wonders,
made itself hollow
so as to take this dead dried up world with it.

It is early, the morning's soft flesh
forms on the horizon, warms
the parched earth, she makes her way
to a small water hole with an antelope,
both inheritors of water, not land.
She sits, afraid,
picks up the wind's song,
her heart a trembling echo.

Singing the song of the broken thread,
the Khoisan woman waits for a message,
that it may float into her ear,
turns the heels of her feet
in the direction where she feels it might blow,
then puts her ear to the earth
so as to understand its flat new sounds,
finely plucked as hunting bows.

The thin tired ground whispers, sends voices:
the sigh of plants, the wail of animals.

She hears the wild olive tree complaining to the earth:
You are too sandy, too loamy, too dry
I can't get a grip.
My fruit has become as dried up black berries.

She hears the thin morning mist complaining
to the wind:
Lift me, lift me
  fishnet of drops.
Take me on your light elbow
  let me drift, soft, over the spiky aloe.

Then the stream complains to the rock:
Just a trickle now, I streamed from high
  kloof and valley to plateau and sea shore
a quick shift of your underbelly
  and I slipped underground.

Poking the earth with a digging stick she remembers
the root of a tree
is food for curing the coughing up of blood,
and tugging up another weed she remembers
the 'lucky plant'.
Burn it, put the ash on your face and
every man will love you.

Closing her eyes the Khoisan woman waits for a message,
like threads in the sky to be climbed, or cobwebs,
or the hands of ancestors helping along the way.

Her grass bushman ancestor,
his face golden in the morning light speaks:
The stars fall when we die. When our hearts fall over
we are not dead but in a deep trance.
We lie tight like ostrich egg beads,
bound together on a strand.
Each bead is part of the circle.

The Khosan woman sits on her haunches,
there is no smoke, no fire,
she longs for the taste of Springbok,
wild honey, to feel cool water.
Adjusting the skin around her waist,
she remembers when the desert lion
dragged a sleeping San woman to the water hole
so he could drink before he ate her,
she thinks of the numb terror as the lion
licked away her tears.
This is how she feels now.

This poem was inspired by writings from Janette Deacon and Craig Foster's: *My Heart Stands in the Hill*, which was originally sourced from records held in the Bleek and Lloyd Archive at the University of Cape Town.

ABOUT THE POETS

Adrienne Silcock's poetry and fiction have appeared widely in the independent press, such as Open Poetry's *Miracle and Clockwork* 2005, *The Clock Struck War* anthology (Mardibooks, 2014) and the Mediterranean Poetry website http://www.odyssey.pm/

Her first novel *Vermin* was published by Flambard. Her second novel *Controlling Aphrodite* was shortlisted for the Virginia Prize 2009. Adrienne's third novel *The Kiss* is published for kindle. She was involved in the *Voices of Women* performance poetry project in conjunction with Wicked Words Poetry, Leeds, and won the 1998 Old Meeting House play-writing competition. She has also self-published poetry pamphlets, *Flight Path,* and *The Fibonacci Sequence.*

www.adriennesilcock.co.uk

Alwyn Marriage has been a university lecturer, chief executive of two NGOs and Editor of a journal. Three of her seven published books have been poetry. She has won and been placed in many competitions, and held Poet in Residence posts with Ballet Rambert and with the Winchester Arts Festival. She holds a research fellowship at the University of Surrey, and gives readings all over Britain and abroad.

Alwyn's latest two poetry collections were *Touching Earth* and *festo* both commissioned by Oversteps before she took over as Managing Editor.

Naming: AD 2006 was performed at the Civil Partnership of friends. Website: www.marriages.me.uk/alwyn.htm

Blog: http://alwynmarriage.wordpress.com.

Andrew McCallum lives and works in Lowland Scotland. He writes in both Scots and English, and his poetry has been broadcast and published widely in Britain and North America. Poems have appeared in dozens of anthologies and in magazines and journals too numerous to list.

Angela France has had poems published in many of the leading journals and has been anthologised a number of times. Her publications include *Occupation* (Ragged Raven Press, 2009), *Lessons in Mallemaroking* (Nine Arches Press, 2011) and *Hide* (Nine Arches Press 2013). Angela is features editor of Iota and runs a reading series, *Buzzwords.*

Anne Macaulay was brought up in rural, northern Scotland but, since meeting her husband in the 70s, has embraced urban life in East London. Proud mother of two grown up children, with 30 years immersed in Education, she now wants to focus more on her writing and loving the Arts!
She has had several poems and a short story published in the last 3 *Loose Muse* anthologies.

Bernie Howley is a Bath-based writer, poet and workshop leader. After working as a research scientist, teacher and homemaker she came to writing, creatively, only recently. To get up to speed she went back to education and picked up a BA in Creative Writing and an MA in Writing For Young People from Bath Spa University. It has been fun and life changing.

Brian Johnstone's work has appeared throughout Scotland, in the UK, north America and Europe. He has published six collections, his latest being *Dry Stone Work* (Arc, 2014). He has read at various international poetry festivals from Macedonia to Nicaragua, and at venues across the UK. Later in 2014 his work will be appearing on The Poetry Archive website.

In 2011 *Robinson* was set to a jazz score by Richard Ingham and performed at venues across Scotland.

Website: http://brianjohnstonepoet.co.uk

Carl Griffin is from Swansea and is Poetry Editor at *Wales Arts Review,* an online magazine. He has recently started *SPIN,* an online poem-swap feedback group. His poetry has been published in magazines such as *Magma, Poetry Wales* and *Anon,* as well as the *Cheval* anthologies.

Cathy Bryant is a former childminder, life model and civil servant. She has won nine literary awards, and co-edited the poetry anthologies *Best of Manchester Poets* vols. 1, 2 and 3. Her latest book *Look At All the Women,* is available from http://www.themothersmilkbookshop.com/.

Cathy's other single author poetry collection is *Contains Strong Language and Scenes of a Sexual Nature.* Cathy has over 200 poems and short stories published in magazines and anthologies.

Elinor Brooks grew up in Edinburgh and now lives in Wiltshire where she teaches English and Creative Writing. Her poems have been shortlisted in competitions and have appeared in magazines and anthologies, on the Big Screen, on fridge magnets and even on an adshel, but most recently in *The Listening Walk* (Bath Poetry Café Anthology) and online at *And Other Poems* ed Josephine Corcoran.

As an active member of Swindon's BlueGate Poets, Elinor has enjoyed being involved in collaborative projects with artists, actors and musicians.

Emma Lee's poetry collection *Yellow Torchlight and the Blues* is available from Original Plus. A pamphlet, *Mimicking a*

Snowdrop was published by Thynks Publishing Summer 2014. She blogs at http://emmalee1.wordpress.com

Freelance creative writing tutor, mentor, poetry editor and writer-in-residence at Swarthmoor Hall. **Geraldine Green** has three poetry pamphlets *The Skin and Passio* (Flarestack), *Poems of a Mole Catcher's Daughter* (Palores). and two collections *The Other Side of the Bridge* and *Salt Road* are both published by Indigo Dreams. Poems and prose have appeared in a variety of anthologies and magazines (online and print) in the UK, Italy and North America. She gained a PhD in Creative Writing Poetry from Lancaster University in 2011.
You can find out more about Geraldine on her blog:
http://geraldinegreensaltroad.blogspot.co.uk

Inua Ellams is an internationally touring poet, playwright and performer. He has been published in eight books of poetry and plays including *Thirteen Fairy Negro Tales* and his first play *The 14th Tale* (a one-man show which he performed) was awarded a Fringe First at the Edinburgh Festival. His third play, *Black T-Shirt Collection* ran at the National Theatre in 2012. He is working on *Barber Shop Chronicles* – a new play, a new pamphlet and a first poetry collection.
He previous poetry publication is *Candy Coated Unicorns and Converse All Stars*

j.lewis is a poet, musician, and Nurse Practitioner. His poetry and music reflect the difficulty and joy of human interactions, and often draw inspiration from his experience in healthcare. When he is not writing, composing, or diagnosing, he is often on a kayak, exploring and photographing the waterways near his home. His work has been published in *Spark: A Creative Anthology Vol 1*

Jennifer A McGowan lives in Oxford. Despite being certified as disabled with Ehlers-Danlos syndrome at age 16, she became a semi-professional mime and performed in five countries till the disability became too much. More recently she has worked as researcher, editor, and writer for a UK company in "devil's advocacy". She has taught both under- and postgraduates at several universities, in subjects as varied as English, history, and heritage studies. Her poems have appeared in many literary journals on both sides of the Atlantic, including *Envoi, Acumen*, and *Agenda* (which also featured her mediaeval calligraphy and illumination); her first chapbook, *Life in Captivity*, is also available from Finishing Line Press. Her work has also been anthologized in *Birchsong* (Blue Line Press, 2012), *A Moment of Change* (Aqueduct Press, 2012), and songs she has written have been recorded on several labels.
www.jenniferamcgowan.com

Jeremy Dixon was born in Essex and now lives in rural South Wales making Artist's Books that combine poetry and photography. His poems have appeared both online and in print. For more information please visit www.hazardpress. co.uk, or follow him on Twitter @HazardPressUK.
Jeremy's work has appeared, or is forthcoming, in *Roundyhouse Magazine, Riptide Journal, Lighthouse Journal, Durable Goods*, and *Really System*, among others.

Jill Sharp is a founder member of Swindon's BlueGate Poets. She tutors for the Open University, runs creative writing workshops and thinks the limerick a greatly underrated poetic form. She posts limerick tweets @LaLimericista
Her work has appeared most recently in *The Listening Walk* (Bath Poetry Cafe), *In Protest* (Human Rights Consortium, London University) Issue 14 of *14 Magazine* (Special edition),

Mslexia, Poems in the Waiting Room and online at *Ink Sweat & Tears* and *And Other Poems.*

Judi Sutherland was made redundant from a career in pharmaceuticals in 2011 and studied for an MA in Creative Writing (Poetry) at Royal Holloway, University of London. She is now writing and teaching poetry and writing a novel.

Poems have been published in *Oxford Poetry, New Statesman, Acumen, the Interpreter's House,* and other magazines.

From midwife to head of a leading archaeological research laboratory – it wasn't until she gave up the day job that **Kate Foley** began publishing. She lives between Amsterdam and Suffolk where she writes, leads workshops and performs.

PUBLICATIONS :

Soft Engineering Onlywomen Press, 1994; *A Year Without Apricots,* Blackwater Press, 1999; *Night and Other Animals* Green Lantern Press, 2002; *Laughter from the Hive* Shoestring Press, 2004; *The Silver Rembrandt* Shoestring Press, 2008; *One Window North* Shoestring Press, 2012; *A Fox Assisted Cure* Shoestring Press 2012

Math Jones was born in London, but lives in Worcester. A pagan in the Old English and Norse tradition, he often writes poetry on the stories and in the metres of that tradition. He also writes more usual verses, narrative, comic, mystical, performing throughout the Midlands and London. A bookseller for many years, he retrained to be an actor, and acts professionally as Math Sams. He is currently understudy to a major role in a West End show.

Two poems in *Melpomene* (anthology); two in *Northern Traditions* (anthology); three in *Ripples* (anthology); individual poems in various magazines: *Decanto, Iota, Be, Hex, Ravenbred,*

Lina, The Wain, Withowinde, Kvasir, Pagan Dawn. Self-published collection: *Eaglespit.*

p.a. morbid edits *The Black Light Engine Room* magazine, and hosts the Middlesbrough based performance night of the same name. Publications: *River Songs* (Ek Zuban Press 2010) *Dark Matter I.* (The Black Light Engine Room Press 2013)

South African **Robin Winckel-Mellish** has lived in the Netherlands for many years and runs a poetry critique group in Amsterdam.

Sam Small is from Glasgow, he writes poetry as a hobby and runs a spoken word night in Glasgow called *Inn Deep Poetry.*

Sarah Lawson was born in Indiana but has lived in London since before decimalisation. Her poems, translations, and book reviews have been published widely. Her translation of Christine de Pisan's *Treasure of the City of Ladies* (1406) was its first English translation (Penguin Classics). Her translation of Moratín's *El sí de las niñas* was performed at the Prince Theatre in Greenwich, and her own play, *Gertrude, Queen of Denmark*, was performed at the Lion and Unicorn in Kentish Town. Her poetry collections are *Below the Surface* (Loxwood Stoneleigh, 1996) and *All the Tea in China* (Hearing Eye, 2005); Hearing Eye has also published her pamphlets, *Twelve Scenes of Malta* and *Friends in the Country*, and a haiku collection, *The Wisteria's Children* (2009).

Simon Brod is a chartered engineer and works in the energy trading division of a large utility. He only started writing in the last few years and is still wondering what took him so long. Simon is a member of a poetry critique group in Amsterdam.

MORE FROM ARACHNE PRESS
www.arachnepress.com

BOOKS

London Lies, ISBN: 978-1-909208-00-1 Our first Liars' League showcase, featuring unlikely tales set in London.

Stations, ISBN: 978-1-909208-01-8 A story for every station from New Cross, Crystal Palace, and West Croydon at the Southern extremes of the line, all the way to Highbury & Islington.

Lovers' Lies, ISBN: 978-1-909208-02-5 Our second collaboration with Liars' League, bringing the freshness, wit, imagination and passion of their authors to stories of love.

Weird Lies, ISBN: 978-1-909208-10-0 WINNER of the Saboteur2014 Best Anthology Award: our third Liars' League collaboration – more than twenty stories varying in style from tales not out of place in *One Thousand and One Nights,* to the completely bemusing.

Mosaic of Air, Cherry Potts, ISBN: 978-1-909208-03-2
Sixteen short stories from a lesbian perspective.

Devilskein & Dearlove, Alex Smith ISBN: 978-1-909208-15-5 A young adult novel set in South Africa. Young Erin Dearlove has lost everything, and is living in a run-down apartment block in Cape Town. Then she has tea with Mr Devilskein, the demon who lives on the top floor, and open a door into another world.

All our books are also available as e-books.

EVENTS

Arachne Press is enthusiastic about live literature and we make an effort to present our books through readings. We showcase our work and that of others at our own bi-monthly live literature event, in south London: *The Story Sessions*, which we run like a folk club, with headliners and opportunities for the audience to join in (http://arachnepress.com/the-story-sessions); but we are always on the lookout for other places to show off, so if you run a bookshop, a literature festival or any other kind of literature venue, get in touch, we'd love to talk to you.

WORKSHOPS

We offer writing workshops, suitable for writers' groups, literature festivals, evening classes – if you are interested, please let us know.